Win-Win Selling

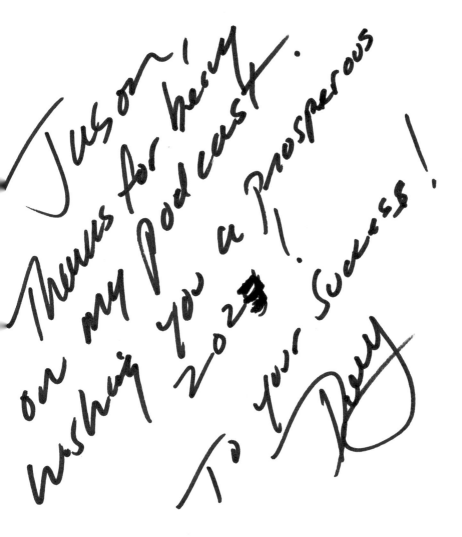

Jason!
Thanks for having
on my podcast.
wishing you a Prosperous
2025!.
To Your Success!

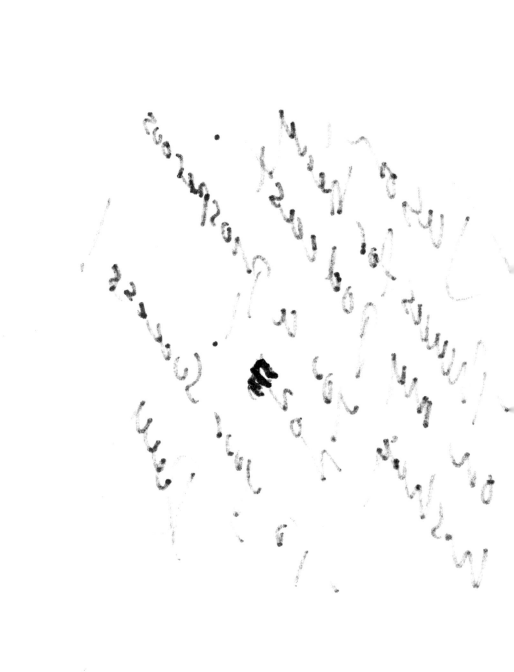

Win-Win Selling

Unlocking Your Power
for Profitability by Resolving
Objections

Doug Brown, CEO, and Sales Expert of
Business Success Factors

Published by Boston Press
20 Portsmouth Avenue
Stratham, NH 03885

Author Doug Brown's email: doug@businesssuccessfactors.com

Limits of Liability and Disclaimer of Warranty
The authors and publisher shall not be liable for the reader's misuse of this material. This book is for strictly informational and educational purposes.

Disclaimer
The views expressed are those of the author and do not reflect the official policy or position of the publisher or Business Success Factors.

Copyright Use and Public Information
Unless otherwise noted, images have been used according to public information laws.

ISBN: 978-0-578-54523-3   Paperback

Contents

ACKNOWLEDGMENTS

I'd like to acknowledge the following people for the inspiration for the material contained within this book.

The first is my father, who brought me into his business when I was three years old. Unbeknownst to me at that age, when I started working, I learned how to sell by being thrust in front of clients immediately. I'm sure back then I was confused. However, upon reflection, I see that it was one of the better experiences I have ever had because I learned to help people, communicate, and negotiate at an early age.

Next, I would like to acknowledge my mother, who was the real salesperson in our family. I still recall her making a living selling Avon when I was four years of age. I listened to her handle objections on price, timing, and "I have to think about it," as I helped her deliver packages, write orders, and collect money for items she sold. The greatest part was figuring out her take of the transaction — her percentage for each sale — as this gave me a sense of what leverage was at an early age. My mother had the drive to communicate, help, and persuade others, and I believe she saw in me that ability.

Sally Nyman, during my teenage years, was like a second mother to me. She was one of the most determined negotiators and best objection handlers I've ever seen. I witnessed her bargain with grocery store management for discounts and perks, as well as in her general interactions with people. She would handle every objection that was tossed her way. Sally was a housewife, and although she had no formalized sales training, she was certainly a professional salesperson.

Steve Nyman, a second father to me, was married to Sally. His mindset helped shape parts of my life. He was a dedicated forward-thinking entrepreneur who made that thought process work in a corporate environment. This later helped me in understanding corporate sales.

Claudia, my wife, who has a methodical and analytical side to her and a way of looking at business and sales, which has challenged me to open my mind. She also has a way of looking at business and sales that has helped and challenged me to grow. She grew up in an environment that was different from mine, and many times, those two upbringings have collided. The process of figuring out how to make that work has been instrumental in my understanding of the psychology behind objections.

My two children, Rebecca and Jacqueline, since the moment of their births have inspired in me a driving force and the desire to be better in my professional and personal life, which in turn has helped tens of thousands of entrepreneurs around the world.

Jackie Morey showed me how to put a book like this together with little stress. Without her easy-to-follow process, this book would have remained thoughts in my head and information only available to those who hired me to teach them.

Russ Whitney, Tony Robbins, Chet Holmes, Andy Miller, and many others are mentors I have learned from to date. Sometimes their lessons have not been easy to grasp, but their knowledge, advice, and accountability have been invaluable to me, and I am forever grateful.

Lastly, our cat, Puck, who comes down to my home office while I am writing, keeps me company, and gives me a good laugh with his antics.

FOREWORD

When Doug Brown asked me to write the foreword to his new book, which you now hold in your hands, my first thought was: *Oh no. Another book on sales and how to sell?* There are so many books written on this topic, that I was afraid it just might be another book repeating the same concepts with a new cover.

As I started to review the book, and then spoke with Doug personally to find out what his motivation was in writing it, Doug gave me a whole different perspective on why he was so motivated and why he wanted to share this invaluable information with the sales world.

Had that discussion not taken place, you might not be reading this foreword from me right now.

Here are a couple points of interest that may enlighten you to the world of information, via books and the written word. I have written thirty books, three of them best sellers. Several have been in print and still selling for over twenty-five years. As authors, we are always approached to write forewords, introductions, or endorsements for other authors.

I don't want to sound stodgy, but I am always suspicious when asked to put my endorsement in any book. Some authors, indeed, do that for more exposure. I decided early on that I would not do that.

So why would I write the foreword to Doug's book? After talking   to Doug and discussing his many years of taking all types of sales training, Doug made a point that had a big impact on me.

He told me that in his past thirty years of sales experience, he had not ever seen or read a book about what he felt was the biggest hurdle for beginners as well as war-torn veteran salespeople. He told me that as a sales trainer for many years he noticed a glaring commonality among beginners and experienced salespeople.

That topic is what Doug's book is all about: *Stop Overcoming Objections! Resolve Them and Close More Sales*. At first, the subject and our talk did not make a big impact on me. After all, I had been involved in the direct sales business for over thirty-five years, and in my mind, I knew all there was to know about the science of selling.

As we spoke more about the topic, Doug caught both my attention and interest to investigate his take on the subject of resolutions as opposed to objections. I thought: *Wow! Doug is definitely onto something here.*

As salespeople, we are usually trained to understand that objections are nothing more than a request for more information. If we don't answer those questions in our initial presentation, then it is inevitable that the question (objection) will come up at the crucial point — the close. The fewer objections we hear at the close, the more likely we will obtain the sale.

Then of course, there are the *smoke-screen objections*. These are responses like:

I/we need to think about it.

What if your company goes out of business?

We never make a decision right away.

I need to check with my spouse.

Most seasoned salespeople will know that when we hear objections like those, it's usually about the money and whether they can afford it, or whether they want to spend it on your product or service.

In this book, Doug takes objections and resolution to a whole new level. This is not an ordinary book at all. It takes one of the most important parts of the science of selling and breaks it down in a unique way that will help you to improve your closing ratio and increase your sales in a big way.

The other thing I like about this book is that Doug used these very strategies to close me, not only on reading it, but then, writing this foreword. His approach was remarkable; it left me with a good feeling and happy to be a part of this great new approach to handling and resolving objections.

Here is one other thing that told me Doug and his new book were onto something: One of my objections with Doug about this book was that it wasn't big enough to be a book. I thought it was more of a special report or a pamphlet.

Doug *resolved* that objection, as well. He explained to me that his goal was not to write a whole book about general sales as most of them are just that. He wanted to focus just on this specialty, which is a thorough understanding and a whole new approach to resolving objections and not overcoming them.

Doug, you've produced a work of art here for anyone in the sales profession, and I'm honored that you asked me to write your foreword — for two reasons:
First, this book is really something to be proud of.

Second, because you asked me to write the foreword, I got all this incredible training for *free!*

Happy reading to all,

Russ Whitney
Best-Selling Author
Inner Voice: Unlock Your Purpose and Passion (Hay House)
Building Wealth (Simon & Schuster)
Millionaire Real Estate Mindset (DoubleDay)
Millionaire Mentor (Dearborne)

INTRODUCTION

Objections have been a part of life since humans first began to communicate. The funny thing is, in all that time, most people haven't learned how to handle these objections.

If you have been in business for any length of time, I'm sure you've encountered an objection or two (thousand!). I'm also sure that you have experienced something that instantly opened your eyes to a world of new possibilities.

This book will build on that premise — that a world of new possibilities will open up for you when you learn how to handle objections easily in a win-win fashion.

You're familiar with the concept of win-win, right?

A win-win is where there is a positive outcome for both, and both people want that outcome.

What you hold in your hands contains game-changing methods for handling objections. Using these methods will result in higher sales conversions and happier customers — both win-wins.

Thousands of people just like you have experienced success with these communication methods. That said, this book requires you to keep an open mind and to be ready to experience a shift in your thinking. When this shift does occur, please don't fight it, as I'm sure you'll be happy with the results.

One of the biggest challenges for most people who sell is that they feel confident about their product or service, and yet, when a buyer comes back with objections — the sale suddenly falls apart.

When I was learning about how to deal with objections, I read countless books and talked to hundreds of professionals. I discovered that when most so-called sales gurus write or teach about overcoming objections, they focus on the objections themselves. They're not digging down to the heart of matter. They're not addressing the psychological underpinnings of the objection. Dealing with the mental makeup behind the objection, though, is the most important ingredient to success.

That's why I wrote this book: because resolving objections effectively is all about understanding the emotional and intellectual foundation of the objection as it relates to the person to whom you are selling.

When you begin to view things from this perspective, you'll see that a successful (or unsuccessful) sale is composed of multiple pieces. There's "what the business can fill" — meaning the product or service — and then there's "what the buyer needs, wants, fears, and must have." It is this latter part — the buyer's needs, wants, fears, and must-haves — that is not always addressed. In my experience, it is this failure to address the personal, subjective demands of the buyer that causes most sales to go sideways.

So, this book was written to give you an understanding of the behaviorism surrounding a sale so that you can build rapport with a buyer (rather than breaking rapport) when resolving objections. And when people are in congruence and in rapport, they'll tend to want to do business with each other.

The following chapters will help business owners, executives, salespeople, and anybody else who must sell to understand that there's more to objections than just: *When this person objects by saying this, you should say this or that.* Canned responses can be useful, but they are not the end-all-be-all technique that makes sales wonderful.

In fact, that canned response you've been taught can (and will, at times) trigger a deeper negative subconscious response within the buyer, which will lead to even more objections.

The bottom line, though, is that objections are nothing to be feared. They should be embraced, because they're part of the natural flow of any human interaction. Just keep in mind that there is more to an objection than words alone. There are human feelings and emotions being expressed in the form of words, and these are not always congruent.

As you head onto this journey, you will learn about the psychology behind objections and how to leverage that knowledge to build rapport and establish connections.

You will learn a process that will help you understand and move forward, resolving objections. You'll master how to address the human needs, wants, must-haves, and fears of the buyer in a win-win fashion. And you will learn that if you follow that process, most of the time you will fare far better than if you didn't.

So, let's jump into the methodology!

CHAPTER 1

IS THE OBJECTION RESOLVABLE?

W e are going to dig deeply into how to resolve objections. Before we do, I want to point something out. Not every objection a potential buyer gives you for not buying will be resolvable. Sometimes it is an objection known as a *non-resolvable* or *immovable* condition. It's important for you to understand the difference.

Condition or Objection?

Years ago, I heard Tom Hopkins, a world-famous sales trainer, ask, "Is the objection an objection, or is it just a condition?"

Why is the answer to that question important? Because if the objection is truly a condition, it's highly unresolvable. If the objection is only an objection, it's resolvable. Defining what a customer says as an objection or a condition is important to establish right away, or you'll be wasting a lot of time trying to sell to someone who cannot buy at that time, even if they genuinely want to do so.

So, what is the difference between the two?

As touched on above, a condition is something that is truly and unfavorably unresolvable. It's a thing that will stop the sale in its tracks. For example, you might be in the process of selling a vacation property with a twenty-year mortgage. The rates are good. It's an excellent offering. There's high value and you can provide high service. There's even high interest shown by the buyer. However, the buyer has just found out that he has pancreatic cancer, and his life expectancy is only two to four months. Treatment may help, but it may not — there's just no way of knowing. The doctors stack the odds at only a ½ percent chance of survival.

As you would expect, the buyer is going to object to the sale, and this objection is not just an objection, but rather a condition. No matter what you do or say, the buyer isn't likely to buy. Sure, there's a slim chance that he may want to buy the property for someone else, but it's a long shot. It's realistic to expect that the buyer isn't going to budge. This objection — this condition — is in all likelihood unresolvable.

Conditions can take many forms. Imagine that you're trying to sell business services or financial services to a client who is going through bankruptcy. Any objections she offers will be conditions because she knows that she could negate her bankruptcy by purchasing something. Or, imagine that you're trying to sell a vacation at an all-inclusive, couples-only resort to a woman who is in the midst of a very nasty divorce with a person who is committed to getting out of the relationship. This is a condition, not an objection, because she is not a couple. The issue is probably unresolvable at that time.

Is the Objection Resolvable?

Timing or lack of money may also be conditions, although some people would argue that they are not.

True conditions are immovable.

However, some conditions that appear to be true can be resolved by re-framing a change in the offer. That change can alter perception of the condition.

Let's say a man, just fell off a boat into the sea, is treading water and is barely able to stay afloat. The condition is he is about to drown.

Buying an automobile from anyone is probably not going to happen at that time no matter how good the offer. Imagine a bad sales response when he brings up the objection to the auto offer:

Sir, you could go down in style. Imagine what the fish are going to be thinking when you arrive in your shiny new Mercedes Benz.

The sale is not going to happen, is it?

But, suppose you change the offer and now were selling a life vest, and a rope line back to the boat. You might make a sale! You see the offer changed, so the immovable condition perception changed and resolved itself unless the man had an immediate desire to end his own life, a death wish, and if so, you have a new condition.

But let's say there is no death wish and you pitch the sale of your life vest and life line back to the boat. The man could still object to the price being too high or object to the timing not being right as he thinks he can tread water and still get back to the boat.

The odds though are likely in your favor that you would make the sale with the life vest and rope and once you made the first sale, and got him safely back into the boat, selling your automobile would also be a possibility.

The point being that true conditions are immovable, but some situations allow you to change the perception of the condition based on the offer.

Thus, you must invest the time and energy to discern each situation.

An objection, then, is everything that is not a condition and can be resolved with a bit of insight and a dash of hard work. As you will learn, a true objection is a fear, or series of fears, set in a frame that can be moved or changed. Your job is to move or change it.

When objections are presented, you must identify whether it is a condition or an objection. Trying to argue a condition is a colossal waste of time, and in the process, you are likely going to break rapport, which is never a good idea.

Conditions and objections can be distinguished through a process of asking lots of questions and by using the formula described in this book. In the process of questioning, if you discover that the objection is a condition; it's time to conclude the sale (in other words, abandon ship — unless you can change the offer to change the perception of the condition). You will save yourself and your client a lot of time and energy by doing so.

If you feel that the condition is time-dependent (as in the bankruptcy case above) you might want to nurture the relationship in the hope that they will purchase your product or service after they're back on their financial feet.

So, with objections versus conditions now well-defined, let's delve into resolving objections.

CHAPTER 2

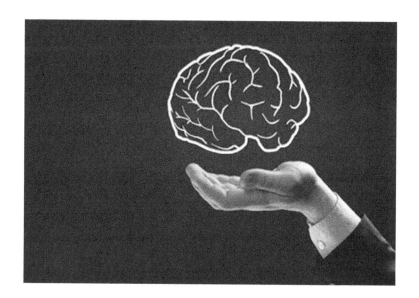

OBJECTIONS ARE LEARNED

Have you ever heard these types of conversations?

"Hey Dad, can I go to the dance this Friday?"

"No, that place will be full of trouble."

"All the other kids are going. Why can't I go?"

"Because I said so."

"That's not a valid reason. I am smart. I can make my own decisions and I want to go to the dance."

"Your sister said the same thing and look how she turned out."

"I am not her."

"You're right. You aren't her. But I said no and no means no."

"You're just trying to control me."

"I am trying to teach you right from wrong."

"You're not fair. I can't wait to move out."

"Coach! Put me in. I'm ready to play."

"Not right now."

"Why not?"

"Because I make the decisions here, and it's not the right time."

"But Coach, I can do it."

"Johnny is playing your position right now. Talk to me later."

"Grandpa, you said you were going to let me know when you were ready to talk about helping my football team. Can we talk now?"

"No, now is not a good time."

"When is?"

"Talk to me in a few weeks."

Perhaps you haven't said those words exactly, but the conversations — or some form of them—are pretty much universal. They are just part of growing up.

But if you consider these conversations from an inquisitive point of view, you'll see that they are classic objections.

"But wait," you say, "these conversations have nothing to do with sales."

On the contrary, my friend. One person (the child) is selling their view, while the other (the adult) is objecting.

A sale needn't always be about money, but it is always about exchanging one value for another.

Thinking more deeply on this subject leads us to these questions:

- *Is it possible that we, as humans, learn from an early age how to create and present objections?*

- *Is it also possible that we, as humans, learn from an early age how to handle objections by crushing, stalling, or controlling them, even if the result is a lose-lose situation?*

The simple (and obvious) answer is yes — objections, and how we deal with them, are learned.

Most people don't think of these conversations as the presentation and handling of objections. Is it any wonder, then, that later in life, people converse like this?

Personal

"Honey, I just got a bonus check from work, and I want to buy a new boat!"

"No way! Are you crazy?"

"But I want a new boat. I work hard, I make the money, and I deserve it! I need a boat to relax."

"You want to spend money on a new boat rather than the children's college fund? I don't think so."

"But I really want a new boat!"

"We already own a boat and it works just fine."

"That old thing?! A new one would be so much better."

"This is a silly conversation and I don't have time for it. It's just the wrong time to buy a new boat."

"No, it's the perfect time."

"I don't think it's in the budget right now."

"We can make a budget for this."

"Why don't we talk about this next year?"

"We could, but now is a better time."

"Let me talk to my father. He just got a new boat and we can see what he thinks."

Business

"So, if you can take delivery within a week, we can wrap it up."

"Let me think about it."

"If we do it now, I can arrange an extra 10 percent off."

"Now might not be the right time."

"When would it be the right time?"

"I don't know, it's just expensive."

"Compared to what?"

"I use suppliers that I am happy with at the moment."

"If you give us a chance, we'll show you how we're better."

"Let me talk to some folks in my office. I'll think about it overnight and then give you a call."

If these examples sound like similar conversations to the one that started this chapter, that's because they are. The adults in these conversations are acting out — or, some might say, continuing to react to — a script they've learned throughout the course of their life. They don't know any other way to handle objections, so they default to what they said and heard during their youth.

We don't have to react in that way. When we know what's going on and why the conversation is going the way it is, we can work to change not only our behavior, but the other person's behavior as well. It's highly probable, then, that such changes will result in a positive outcome for all.

Now that we've established that the types of conversations, we're likely to encounter during the sales process come from behaviors learned and ingrained during one's lifetime, let's examine another aspect: where objections come from. Armed with these two ideas — learned behavior and the source of objections — we'll learn how to resolve sales reluctance successfully.

CHAPTER 3

WHERE DO OBJECTIONS COME FROM?

In this chapter, we'll learn:

1. How objections form
2. How to deal with objections before they even come up

Let's talk about Superman for a moment. The Man of Steel is a pretty powerful guy — virtually indestructible. But what happens when he's exposed to kryptonite, the radioactive element from his home planet

Krypton? He loses his "super power" and becomes just a man—for him, weak and powerless.

"How does this relate to sales?" you might ask. Well, just as kryptonite is to Superman, objections can be to the sales professional, entrepreneur, and business owner.

But it doesn't have to be that way. Objections or even rejections are not to be feared.

Years ago, I was selling business services from live, virtual presentations via the worldwide web. Some people call these webinars. Our services literally and positively increased a business' revenues and profits. I was brand new to selling though a webinar and my close rate was over 50%! That was really high considering our industry competition was 7-12%. At the time, my company couldn't figure out why I was doing so well, and I couldn't either. My close rate stayed consistent for over five years while I was working there.

Today, I understand that part of my success was that I was not concerned if people rejected me because I was playing win-win. I showed up as my authentic self and tried to give the webinar attendees what they needed.

It's not technique only that lies at the foundation of successful sales, it's caring about people and helping them meet their needs, and when your mission to serve is super strong, then your fear of rejection is lowered.

So, let's set aside fear for the moment, and look at objections as a normal part of the sales process.

NOTE: For simplicity's sake, we will refer to two parties throughout this text: *the seller and the buyer.* Even though these terms may not always describe the complex relationship between salesperson and client, they help us understand the two sides of the interaction.

Key: The first key to dealing with objections is to understand what creates them. Once you see how objections form in the buyer's mind, you can set about identifying the most common objections and how to deal with them.

Insight: Objections form primarily out of fear. An objection comes about because there's a feeling of uncertainty from the receiving party.

In other words, the seller may be saying something that is causing the buyer to feel uncertain and out of control, or the buyer may already feel the fear prior to meeting the seller. Either way, this leads the buyer to feel that they could be compromised or hurt in some way and this causes them to shut down and go on the defensive.

It's crucial to understand that objections can grow from even tiny fears.

When the buyer feels any measure of fear, they strive to regain their uncertainty by making an objection. So, Fear = Uncertainty = Objections.

This chain of events happens primarily when the seller is focused on their own goals, rather than on the buyer's goals.

The interesting thing about all this is that, to protect themselves, the buyer then tries to do the same thing as the seller: they try to "sell" their position. If both sides are positioning, they're locked in   a metaphorical emotional arm-wrestling match, which we'll call an *arm lock* — in which no one can move. The inner perception of an arm lock tells the buyer that the salesperson doesn't care. As a result, *trust*, *respect*, and *like* will be lost.

Buyers rarely purchase anything from sellers they do not trust, respect, and like.

An Objection Is an Emotion and a Behavior

We've established that fear leads to uncertainty, and uncertainty leads to objections.

The interesting thing about that cause-and-effect is that the objection doesn't have to be logical. That's because an objection is a behavior fueled by emotion, and emotion is energy in motion, even if it's not logical. Always remember that objections are emotion based.

The buyer's reaction to the emotion they are feeling (fear) causes them to object to protect themselves from uncertainty and possible harm (physical, mental, financial, and so on). So, in reality, an objection isn't an objection — it's just protection the buyer uses for themselves. It's like our natural tendency to cover our head when we hear a loud noise. We don't even think about it; we just do it.

Once we understand what an objection is (an uncertainty based on fear) and why it forms (to protect the buyer from harm), we can deal with the situation more effectively. When dealing with the emotion that underlies all objections, it's important to realize that while fear usually manifests in the present moment, its origin is usually rooted in the past or the future.

If it's the former, the buyer has experienced fear and possibly harm in the past. If the seller says or does something that trips a memory of that fear, then that fear reveals itself in the now. That fear may have been present long before the seller even knew the buyer.

For example, let's say the buyer objects to the amount of money required for the sale. We know they are speaking from a feeling much deeper than this simple statement. Perhaps as a child, they were constantly chided for spending money foolishly, and now they fear spending money will be a foolish endeavor. Perhaps they hear a parent's voice in their head: *What's the matter with you? Why do you throw money away?* This fear was not caused by the seller or the product.

Regardless, when that memory is tripped, the buyer travels back in time — figuratively speaking, of course — and drags the fear into the present moment. The objection comes from a younger version of the buyer who has been brought up to think a certain way. This can also happen if the buyer is pre-framing too far into the future. This simple act can cause them anxiety, and they may pull that anxiety into the present — into the sales call, presentation, or meeting.

Thus, if the seller poses a hypothetical or "what-if" statement, and that hypothetical seems scary to the buyer, that future fear can be pulled into the present and cause objections to form. Resolving these fears, be they from the past or future, comes through understanding how they form and what objections may result.

Selling scenarios or situations are different, and from industry to industry may differ, but fears and objections from industry to industry are usually similar or even universal. If you are selling music, for example, the fears and objections generated will usually be similar to the fears and objections generated if you're selling marketing, or if you're selling automobiles.

Again, all objections are based on *fear* — on the potential buyers' side. Whether it be defined as fear, discomfort, wanting control back, or feeling like they are not in control, if the seller fails to address fears and objections, the situation can escalate from a discussion to locking horns in a full-on fight.

If so, the buyer and seller are no longer dealing with objections; they're engaged in a conflict. This situation is no longer about first emotions — fears — but now, because of conflict, additional emotions have been piled on top.

That's when buyers and sellers become confused about how to resolve the issues, because the conflict is suddenly about rivalry rather than just fear.

The Core of All Objections

Many experts claim that there are only six objections. Others claim there are five or even seven. Contrary to those ideas, I have found that there are many different types of objections.

That said, they can all be reduced into general categories, like time:

> *I don't have enough time.*

> *I'm not sure if I will have enough time.*

> *I'm not sure we can make the time.*

Or money:

> *I can't afford it.*

> *I don't think I will have the money.*

> *I don't know how I'm going to acquire the money.*

> *I'm not sure we have the budget.*

> *I'm not sure there's going to be a budget appropriated.*

Or even time *and* money!

> *We must wait until next year to figure out if the budget is going to be appropriated.*

Obviously, there are different flavors of objections. Because of that, I don't personally subscribe to the idea that there are a certain finite number of objections.

As stated previously, though selling processes may differ from industry to industry, the objections are often similar, regardless of what you are selling.

There is one addition to this rule; *sub-niche objections.*

Sub-niche objections are specific to an industry niche and have their own specialized terminology.

For example, if I were selling in the marketing industry, the buyers would come up with *sub-niche objections* that would never come up if I were selling, say, telecommunications products like landlines and data.

Sub-niche objections exist because of different history, processes, terminology, and business practices specific to one individual industry.

In telecommunications, for example, one may object to the fear of having their communications being knocked out of service by changing providers due to a change in an FOC "Firm Order Commitment" DATE.

But regardless of the industry, the common nucleus of all objections is the same.

So, if I had to answer the question, "How many types of objections are there?" I would say there's only one real objection: discomfort (which is formed by a small or large fear).

Insight: The individual who is objecting is simply trying to alleviate some discomfort.

This is an important point. It's what distinguishes my methods from the methods of others who talk about "overcoming objections." To put a finer point on it, the primary objection from which all other objections stem is that the buyer is trying to alleviate discomfort by regaining some level of certainty.

Why?

So that they can decide without feeling: *Oh, if I made this decision, something negative could come of it.*

Key: The more that the seller can disperse, alleviate, and lower the fear on one end of the spectrum, and then build up buying confidence on the other end, the fewer objections they will tend to hear.

Fear — Where Does It Come From?

The origin of all fear comes from the way we operated as a species for thousands of years. For example, most people are, to varying degrees, afraid of the dark. This fear manifests most frequently at night. They may not feel or acknowledge the fear in their house, but chances are, they feel it when they are in unfamiliar surroundings. Why is that?

It's because way back when our more primitive, reptilian brains ruled our behavior, we had to be aware of the many predators that hunted in the dark of night. Back then, we were not the top of the food chain, and those many predators that stalked at night came after us. Add to that the fact that the dark of night took away our primary means of sensing the world, our sight, and it's easy to see that our ancestors had good reason to be afraid of the dark, or at least leery of it.

That powerful fear and the self-preservation reaction that accompanied it was passed down through the generations to us today. Though we are no longer hunted by nocturnal predators, and artificial light keeps the dark at bay, the instinct to fear remains.

CHAPTER 4

WE ALL HAVE BEEN FRAMED

Wikipedia defines frames as "a set of concepts and theoretical perspectives on how individuals, groups, and societies organize, perceive, and communicate about reality." This is a nice definition if you're a psychologist or a social scientist, but you may be wondering what it has to do with sales. Well, believe it or not, it has everything to do with sales.

In fact, frames are a must if you want to understand the basics of dealing with objections. In its simplest form, a frame is a mental representation of how a person thinks and acts. Once you understand a person's frame, you're better prepared to resolve any objections that they may raise.

The key to the process is remembering that it's all about how a person thinks and acts. When we consider the individual's perspective, feelings, wants, needs, fears, and desires, we can be more open and make a deeper connection with our client.

The challenge for most salespeople is that they have been taught to crush objections with certain specific techniques or skills. They forget that the social frame — the one that governs their thoughts, as well as the thoughts of their clients — is already set.

For example, if the client has a *dominant* personality, their frame will be set up as dominant. This might seem obvious, but it means that they want to be in charge all the time. So even if you give them all the logical reasons in the world to buy, if you don't address the dominant frame, they may feel as if they did not make the decision and thus, do not buy. Why? They feel they are not in charge. The same thing happens if the person is an *influencer* — the type of person who likes to be sociable and entertaining.

Frames — They Are Not Just for Paintings

There are social frames in every society. Within those societies, every person has a unique frame from which they operate. Each person — and each frame — is influenced by social norms, upbringing, religion, gender, and a whole host of other factors. A buyer might be framed by an ethnic heritage, such as a large Italian family. Or, they might be framed by their unique experience as a woman in or from a Latin American culture. Your seller has a frame, and so do you.

Though it would be nice to understand them all, studying each and every frame would be a massive undertaking, and would be extremely valuable if you had the time, but if not, remember you really must understand the basics.

The most important thing to remember is that a frame is a window through which all individuals look to determine how they think, feel, and act.

Because frames are so influential, they can stop a person from resolving an objection quickly. What's more, the person won't even know that it's the frame that's holding them up.

For example, I recently witnessed a sales presentation between a salesperson from the United States and two potential buyers from Israel. The product was a business mastermind event — a gathering of people to share ideas and receive training on a high level.

The two potential buyers from Israel wanted the salesperson from the United States to sell them two tickets for the price of one. In their country, and in their industry, it is common practice to allow the second person to attend a live event. The rule in their country is that the first person pays full price, and the second person is invited as a guest of the first.

This is normal business practice, and everyone in their country does it that way.

In the United States, this is not common practice. Typically, people pay two separate entrance fees, or one higher entrance fee for a group. The salesperson's frame was set in this context. Can you see the challenge in this situation?

The potential buyers were objecting to the process — having to pay for two tickets — because their frame was set in a different context. Remember, that their objection stemmed from a socially constructed frame, not the actual price of the tickets. Essentially, they were saying one thing but meaning another.

Unfortunately, the salesperson was using techniques based on price to persuade the potential buyers that this was a great deal, which it was, and that they needed it to grow their business, which they did. The potential buyers kept objecting, and the inexperienced salesperson kept chasing that objection with no success. The spoken objection was a smokescreen for the real objection, which rose from a cultural frame.

The potential buyers were operating through a frame that told them that they were being deceived or slighted — missing out on the customary two-for-the-price-of-one — so they threw up the first objection they could think of: price.

Both potential buyers were highly dominant personalities with dominant frames, and I could tell that their defenses were up. I asked to step in and promptly changed the subject. We briefly talked about Israel. We talked about common practices there. We talked about travel.

As I asked them questions, gathered information, gave them answers and rewards, and asked more questions — the same formula I teach in this book — their dominant frame turned to curiosity. As soon as this happened, they were open to a new approach and eventually ended up purchasing two tickets for $42,500, paid in full. That's a successful sale.

In his book, *Pitch Anything*, Oren Klaff writes that every meeting, every pitch, and every presentation is a social encounter governed by a point of view, a perspective, or a position — what we've been calling a frame. The salesperson comes with a frame and the customer comes with a frame.

The thing is, different frames don't combine or mix when they meet. Rather, they collide, and the strongest frame always wins. It's kind of like a psychological game. In the case described above, the curiosity frame was stronger. When the customers shifted to that frame, their fear decreased, their buying confidence increased, and I could make a sale.

The point I want to make in this chapter is that you don't have to become a frame expert, although that would be invaluable. Rather, you must be aware that people come into the sales process with preset frames. When you prepare to sell, or persuade anyone to buy anything, ask yourself: *From what frame, or frames, may the potential buyer operate?*

When you've identified the possible frames they may be carrying, realize that this will be their go-to position, or their default, so to speak. Humans fall back on their default frame because their brains are wired to protect them. Oren Klaff calls this reaction the "croc brain," while neuroscientists refer to it as the reptilian brain.[1] The reptilian brain controls the body's autonomic functions, such as heart rate, breathing, body temperature, and balance. It is this part of the brain that controls our fight-or-flight response and reacts first (usually without our knowing it) when we are introduced to new things, be they physical or mental.

These reactions are left over from a time long ago when we were not the top of the food chain and had to defend ourselves just to survive. Our brains adapted so that we could identify friend or foe without really thinking; the primitive part of our brains just did it for us.

Even though we've come a long way since those early days, the primitive part of our brain still operates the same way, says Klaff. It still snaps to fight-or-flight when faced with something new. Thankfully, the limbic system (emotions) and the neo-cortex (thinking) help us govern our reptilian reactions. If we didn't, the world would be a different place.

When you're making a presentation or pitching an idea, the customer's brain automatically goes through the reptilian processes of survival and aggression. If they feel threatened in some way, even if they can't perceive or even understand

---

[1] Klaff, Oren. *Pitch Anything: An Innovative Method for Presenting, Persuading, and Winning the Deal.* McGraw-Hill, 2011.

the threat, they will react on instinct and object in order to feel safe again.

The interesting thing about this process, and the thing that you always need to keep in mind, is that they may react in a way that is not even related to the true objection. For example, they may throw out something like price or convenience, or say they must talk with a higher-up, when what they're truly objecting to is all the paperwork that this will generate. In reality, they may not know why they're objecting.

Their reptilian brain is simply reacting to something you said or did that seems threatening in some way. When this happens, the clients are operating through a default frame, and that frame and what the person selling is saying is causing discomfort and fear.

A default frame is one reason I recommend against using corporate buzzwords, such as *needed agenda*. For many buyers, these words trigger a frame constructed in work environments both present and past. Layered in their history, this frame can evoke years of feeling threatened, afraid, or exhausted. Once present, this frame is difficult for both the seller and buyer to control.

The concept of the reptilian brain and its automatic reactions doesn't just apply to potential buyers or customers, according to Klaff. It applies to you, too. It's why one of the first rules of handling an objection is to take a breath and relax. If you don't control your reptilian brain, your fight-or-flight instinct will take over, and you'll find yourself in a duel of the minds with the other person.

So, to sum up, people carry psychological frames with them through which they relate and react to the world around them. From a sales context, the frame through which they look determines how they perceive you as a salesperson, as well as what you can offer.

In order to handle objections effectively, you should strive to understand what frame they are operating in, and then help them change to a more receptive frame. You should also realize that the potential purchaser isn't likely going to operate from the logical part of their brain — at least not at first. Rather, they are going to default to the reptilian brain, which is going to push them into the frame of fear. Your job, then, is to stay out of that frame yourself by breathing, relaxing, and thinking before you act or speak, and then to help the customer switch to a more amenable frame.

CHAPTER 5

BELIEFS AND VALUES CAN CREATE OBJECTIONS TOO

I talk at length about moral obligation at various places in this book because it is an important part of being a good salesperson. If you don't recall, or haven't yet read about it, don't fret, I'll review it here.

In a general sense, moral obligations are classified as beliefs, or even values. In a more specific sense, your moral obligation is a part of you that feels so strongly about what you do and sell that you are genuinely convinced that your client's life would be better if they had your product or service, and that their life would be worse if they did not acquire it. Therefore, it is your sincere moral responsibility: "you owe it to them" to make sure they purchase it.

Your moral obligation for your clients and for yourself motivates you to go to any respectable lengths, while still staying in rapport, to make your clients understand your position. This only comes from a place that is win-win. When you position yourself to achieve a win-win, the concepts of respectability, as in *any respectable lengths*, and rapport, as in *staying in rapport*, become your primary concerns.

Taken together, the concepts of respectability, rapport, and win-win fuel that moral obligation mentioned earlier. Thus, if you don't have a sense of moral obligation for your product and service, your client, and yourself, it might be time to look for something else to sell . . . preferably something you believe in.

Contrary to popular consensus, believing in what you sell is extremely important. If you don't believe in what you sell, you will likely cave in, hide, or become argumentative when an objection is posed. And if you haven't heard an objection yet, rest assured that you will at some point.

Remember, an objection is an integral part of the whole sales process. There's a better than average chance that an objection will occur. That's why it's important to be prepared and to approach your client with a sense of high moral obligation.

Granted, there may be a few times that no objections are posed. These occasions are so rare, however, that when they do occur, you may be left asking yourself: *What just happened?* or: *Why didn't the client have any objections?* This can lead to feelings of doubt that leave you questioning if the sale will stick. Will there be buyer's remorse?

Buyer's remorse is always a possibility. But you will also close sales from time to time that are just fine and do stick, even if the client doesn't object. However, these cases are not the norm, no matter how well you have prepared, how great your presentation is, or how great you close.

Just the other day I closed a sale during which the client didn't object at all. It was a smaller sale for me — $17,000 USD — conducted over the phone, as the client lives 1100 miles away. I was representing someone else's brand and selling their product, and the sale went through without a hitch in only about an hour. I asked a simple closing question: *"Would you like to move forward with this now?"*

She said yes. I took her information and processed her payment, and then invested some time with her after the sale, building additional value, going through next steps, and celebrating with her. She thanked me, and we hung up. That was it. It was a normal one-call close that I do almost every day.

Twelve and a half hours later, I got an email from the client asking, "Are you for real?" Evidently, she had gone searching for me on the internet but couldn't find much information about me on social media. This is in no way unusual because some people don't know how to find social media profiles.

I was a bit confused by the client's email because I had given her my LinkedIn profile, cell phone number, and personal IM.

On top of that, I was representing a brand with which she already had done business. She even had to initially fill out a questionnaire when she requested the appointment to talk with me. There was familiarity and some trust already built into the relationship from the brand.

Even with all that, she developed a fear that she might have been sold something by someone who took her money and disappeared.

Where did that come from?

Fortunately, I do a lot of qualification before I make an offer (you want to do this too). I do that with questions and formulas introduced and explained in this book. The questions are used to find out about the client's beliefs and values.

During our conversation (throughout which I used those questions), I discovered that she has a high need for control in everything she does. When she isn't in control, she feels frightened and doubtful. She told me that it comes from childhood experiences with her parents. I also discovered that she had been taken advantage of by unethical salespeople in the past.

Based on these and other clues, I knew that objections might come up after the sale. That's why I gave her my LinkedIn profile, personal cell phone number, and personal IM right away. I wanted to show her that I was not the same as those who had dumped her in the past and to demonstrate to her, I wasn't going to run away.

All my efforts weren't enough. So here we were after the sale: her with an objection that needed to be resolved and the need to maintain the delicate balance so as to not to crush or overcome her objection, but to resolve it in a win-win fashion.

But what exactly was she looking for? This is the magic question all salespeople should ask before reacting. Turns out, she was seeking certainty and security, and she wanted to test that premise.

She sent her message at 11:18 p.m. my time. That is late at night for most people, but I happened to be online at the time. The first thing I did was send her a message right back. I didn't wait. I responded immediately. How many salespeople without a moral obligation will send you a message back at 11:30 at night?

The message went like this:

Hi (first name),

This is Doug. Wow, you are up late tonight! Thanks for the message. You seem like you are seeking some more information on my profile. Can you please tell me more specifically what you are seeking?

She typed back within minutes.

I cannot find a lot about you online, so I am seeking profiles.

Within a minute, I typed back to her.

Hi (first name),
I am not sure what specific profiles you are seeking.
Attached is my bio in the event this is what you are looking
for. I sent a connection request to you today on LinkedIn
and saw that you reviewed my profile but have not
connected with me.

I am not feeling 100 percent — have a touch of the flu or
something (started this afternoon) (kids had it first...guess
it's my turn) — so I am going to bed.

Let me know if you have any questions, etc., and I will
address in the morning.

To Your Success!

Doug

What I want you to understand is that my response is not award winning. Some salespeople would pick it apart, saying, *"Doug, you could have used this NLP process or this type of reclose technique."* And all that is true. I could have, but I did not need to because I was being genuine and human. She knows that even though I had the flu, I cared enough about her to respond to her. I gave her more information about myself and the knowledge that she was important enough to me to recognize that she had checked my LinkedIn profile. I gave her certainty that I was there, and this was the first step she was seeking.

Hopefully, it is obvious from this example that you must care about the people to whom you sell, and you must have the moral obligation to serve them. This comes from your beliefs and your values. No matter what level of sales skill you possess, or how famous you or your clients are, you will always face objections and sales challenges.

At the time of this writing, the sale is still intact.

I've said it before, but it's worth saying again: Remember, things happen because you are dealing with people who live by beliefs and values. You have yours and they have theirs. At times, beliefs and values will be complementary to one another, and at times they will not.

This poses the question: what exactly are beliefs and values, and where do they come from?

Firstly, rest assured that this is not going to be a long explanation. Yes, psychologists, doctors, and gurus devote entire books to this subject because it can be very involved and have deep subject matter. For this book, I want to illustrate the basics to you, so you can grasp and understand the concept.

Simply stated:

1.   Beliefs are thoughts and thought patterns that the individual accepts as true.

2.   Values are ingrained beliefs which are accepted as a
      standard of worth.
3.   The more important the perception of the individual
      need for the belief, the stronger the value to that
      person.

Beliefs and values are formed from the individual's life
experiences, be they bad or good. Because of this, beliefs
and values can and do change over time. One major
influence on how beliefs and values change is whether they
are held by the individual as weak, medium, or strong. The
stronger the belief or value, the more the individual will
hold their position — even if that position makes no sense
to the general population.

War makes little sense to most of the world's population.
Death comes from it, but we still see wars happening over
time. Why? Because the stronger the belief or value for the
need for war, the more the individual will hold their
position. When these held positions are opposing between
people, this will create discord and conflict.

As it applies to sales, beliefs and values play a large part in
determining how a person will react to your offer. In some
cases, your offer will likely contain something that runs
contrary to their beliefs and values. When this happens —
and it will — an objection is not far off. These objections,
as mentioned above, can be weak, medium, or strong, like
the beliefs and values on which they are based. These
objections can be so strong, in fact, that they may create
irrational fears and behaviors.

Strangely enough, even your own beliefs and values can cause an objection to appear. That's right—you can unconsciously cause the customer to object just by how you present your own beliefs and values. Let me explain.

We all have life experiences. These life experiences form our beliefs. They can come from cultural influences, gender differences, societal expectations, how you were framed while you were raised, and much more. Over time and with much repetition, these beliefs turn into values if you accept them.

Let's say you grew up in an environment where you were taught not to expect the purchase of expensive things. Perhaps your parents were frugal, or had a hard time making ends meet. Regardless of the reasons, you learned not to pay too much for anything, or that you just can't afford high-priced items.

Fast-forward many years, and here you are, selling a high-end training program, a luxury automobile, or a simple item like an expensive lamp. In the back of your mind, you might be thinking: *Wow! I wouldn't pay that much for this item.*

Because of this, you may routinely hear the objection, "It's just too expensive," or one of its myriad variations.

Or, perhaps you grew up in an environment where everything was a negotiation. You believe that you should always receive something more, regardless of the initial offer. During your sales presentations, then, you consistently hear, "Is that the best you can do?" or "Can you throw in something else?" from potential buyers.

Where do you think this comes from?

It comes from your beliefs and values influencing your customer's beliefs and values. Your thinking invoked your language and actions, which persuaded your customer's thinking. Your beliefs and values affected your customer's beliefs and values.

At this point, you might be thinking, "Oh come on! Their cultural background is the same as mine. They lived in the same neighborhood as I did. They're the same sex and went to the same schools and religious organizations as I did. That's why they're acting like me, not because of some unconscious projection of my beliefs and values."

I do admit, that's entirely possible. But think about this: is it also possible that you are thinking about how you would react to the offer — *it's too expensive* — and possibly using language patterns that are invoking the objection?

It's completely possible, and even probable. Your brain is like a radio transmitter that broadcasts your thought signal for everyone to tune in to.

Ask yourself: *Is my transmitter set to the objection frequency?*

You might be thinking right now: *So, Doug, are you telling me that I'm broadcasting my beliefs and values to my potential buyers, and that because I believe them to be true, I might be saying things that are causing the customer to feel that way too?*

Yes, that's exactly what I'm saying. We unconsciously — and sometimes consciously — defend our beliefs and values every moment of our life. We do this through our words and actions. And because we're doing this without realizing it, it's easy to project or communicate our beliefs and values to the customer on the other side of the conversation without knowing that we're doing it.

So, if you are hearing the same objection frequently, it's likely that you are not covering the objection upfront, and it's equally likely that you are causing the objection to come up through your actions and words.

Begin with yourself.

Ask yourself: *Do I value what I sell?*

Is the sale worth the money, effort, or time the buyer must invest? Do I see that people must buy right now for their benefit or that they can wait?

These attitudes are transmitted to the buyer. Recently, I received an email asking if I wanted to hire a ghostwriter. For a limited time of thirty days, I could receive 85 percent off ghostwriting services. Now, this ghostwriter could be the best ghostwriter in the world. Maybe they just wrote a celebrity's memoirs. Regardless, the 85 percent discount offer invoked a thought in me based on my belief system that if somebody is going to drop their price by that amount, the end product can only be a really bad book.

Maybe this writer was taught as a child never to take and always give. Maybe they value helping people move forward and they do not want to charge a lot because at one time they did not have money, and they value making ghostwriting affordable for all. They could possibly be a billionaire and not need the funds. Whatever the reason, this offer still communicated to me a lack of confidence in the writer's skills and my objection of "I fear the quality of their work will cause harm to my reputation" and my decision of "not for me" kicked in.

As difficult as this concept that you may be causing the objection within your potential buyer may be to accept, the solution is infinitely easier. All it takes to counteract your beliefs and values is first an awareness and then a strong focus of moral obligation toward your customers and your offerings.

Recently, an elite saleswoman came to me and told me that most of her leads were all "broke and broken." Normally she was at the top of her sales team, but she had just started with a new client and was selling their training program to potential buyers, which included working with top trainers. She was struggling to compete.

The company hired me to help and I took on some leads to understand their potential buyers and offerings. So, there I was — the new guy, way ahead of her, and because she was so competitive, it drove her crazy.

She repeated that all her leads were "broke and broken," and then asked me what I was doing that was so different from what she was doing. I knew that her leads were not broke and broken because I was calling upon the same leads and making four times as many sales as she was at that time.

I asked her what she meant by "broke," and she told me that most of her leads were struggling financially and had no expendable cash. Then I asked her what she meant by "broken," and she told me that most of her leads did not possess the business sense that she did.

Finally, I asked her if she believed that her leads needed access to the top trainers to understand her business sense and be successful, or if they could succeed at the level they wanted without the top trainers.

She paused for a moment, and then said, "Wow! I didn't think of that. I guess I believe that top trainers are nice to work with, but they could be successful with just a good trainer."

I explained to her that she is an elite sales professional with decades of business experience, and it is doubtful her leads command that same level of skill. I went on to say that I believed her leads did need the top trainers to bring them to the next level, and that it was my moral obligation to help them obtain the best so that they did not unnecessarily struggle for years. I did not want them making mistakes that would cost them mounds of stress, and the offering we were selling was the best path.

I shared that my concern for the client was the main reason I was outselling her, and unfortunately, she was broadcasting her beliefs and values — that the top-tier trainers were not necessary — onto her leads. Because of her projection, the leads thought that they needed a trainer but weren't ready to pay for the best of the best. So, they objected based on cost, saying they could not afford it.

The leads were not broke or broken. I then showed her that her customers were in fear, and that she, the saleswoman, was invoking the objections through her language patterns and demeanor. The customer's fear, coupled with the unconscious expression of the saleswoman's values, was enough of an uncomfortable feeling to make the customer object.

She paused, thought for a moment, and said, "Thank you. I guess my beliefs and values are standing in the way of their success." In the next two days, she made four new sales!

Monitor Your Beliefs and Values

You as the seller can, indeed, create an objection, and cause it to appear because of your beliefs and values. So how do you know if this is what's happening? And if it is, how do you make it stop? The answer is simple.

If you are hearing the same objection repeatedly, ask yourself: *Do I think their objection is valid?*

Then, be honest with yourself. If even a tiny part of you says yes, then you believe it too.

Once you realize that even just a tiny part of you believes that their objection is valid, you can work to change that belief. It's that simple.

If you are hurting your potential buyer, your moral obligation to yourself and to your customer is to challenge that belief head on and find a way to see it differently.

People used to believe that if one sailed too far away from land, their boat would just fall off the edge of the earth, and they would never be seen again. They believed that the world was flat. Obviously, we do not believe that anymore. Our beliefs changed.

At one time, people believed that television was a fad. People believed that the automobile would never replace the horse as the main mode of transportation. If someone had a bad heart wound, people believed they were destined to die quickly. And yet all these beliefs have changed over the course of the last hundred years.

Your beliefs and values can change, too, if you want them to. All it takes is a bit of honesty, a change to your perspective and habits, and a moral obligation to yourself and your customers.

So, to reiterate, if you hear the same objection multiple times, just ask yourself: *Do I think this is true too?*

Be honest with yourself, and if even a tiny part of you says yes, you believe it too. Then, challenge that belief and work to see the other side of the issue. Keep repeating that process until the belief has shifted. When you've successfully done that, you can head off the objection in your presentation, and it won't occur often, or it may not occur at all.

CHAPTER 6

THE RULES FOR
RESOLVING OBJECTIONS

In this chapter, we will learn:

Insights and rules for resolving objections

When you carefully follow the trail of your objections, you will notice that they come to you in order of the potential buyer's priority. By tracking these priorities over time, you will be able to identify which objections are more likely to come up first. With that knowledge, you'll then be able to head them off before they rear their ugly heads.

How, exactly, does one accomplish such?
You do it in your positioning and your presentation.

We'll talk about how to adjust that in a bit, but for now, let's revisit where fear comes from.

Insight: If the buyer has their thoughts in the past or the future and they are uncomfortable, then the buyer is pulling negative emotions into the present, where they create objections.

By objecting, the buyer is trying to regain some semblance of *certainty*. Certainty is a basic human need related to *safety*.

To illustrate how certainty and safety apply to priorities and the selling process, put yourself in the following situation: You are walking through the woods when, suddenly, you hear a bear growl close by. Alarmed by the prospect of being *Ursus arctos'* next meal, your safety immediately becomes your top priority.

You are going to do whatever it takes to regain the certainty that you are safe from the bear's claws—run away, climb a tree, swim a river, whatever.

The sales scenario is no different. If the buyer feels that their safety is threatened, they are going to do whatever it takes to regain that safety. And while they probably won't climb a tree or swim a river, they will pose objections as a defense against the fear they feel.

But imagine if you could ask that bear a question:

"Excuse me, Mr. Brown Bear, are you planning on eating me?"

"No," says Mr. Brown Bear, "I'm just calling my wife. I am lost, and every time I get lost in the woods, she thinks I am sneaking off to find a girlfriend."

How would you feel then? Your safety isn't in question anymore, so it's not necessary to climb a tree or swim a river. A simple question diffused the whole issue.

The sales scenario is no different. If you can persuade the buyer either to respond to and ask the right questions, they won't need to object to regain their safety.

The important question then becomes, "How do you guide the buyer to move from an objection to a question?" The answer to that question can be found in the rules for handling objections.

The Nine Rules for Handling Objections

Sellers are often taught that the first thing they need to do is *overcome* the objection to keep the sale moving. I argue that that's not the right first step.

I've said it several times already, and I do not want you to think that I am preaching, but it's paramount to understand that when you are presented with an objection, the objection's coming from a place of fear and your potential buyer is uncomfortable.

Insight: Fear is not a false expectation that appears real. Fear is a real expectation that appears real, and a person who feels fear is experiencing something that is uncomfortable for them. It doesn't appear real to them; it is real to them!

The buyer feels something. The buyer feels *fear of something*, and it is real to them. The reaction to that fear is to object. Just because they object, it does not mean there is no possible win-win sale if you get them answering and asking the right questions.

So how do you guide the buyer to move from an objection to a question? There are nine rules and here is the first success step.

Rule #1: Breathe and Relax

"Why breathe and relax?" you ask. Because if you don't breathe and relax, you are going immediately to try to conquer or overcome the objection, and that is playing you-win-and-they-lose.
The worst thing you can do is try to overcome the objection right off the bat.

Insight: Objections do not need to be overcome. In fact, most people do not want their point of view invalidated.

Is this a new insight for you? It is for most people.
Here's another.

Insight: Rather than trying to overcome the buyer's
objections, look instead for a win-win.

Yet how are most salespeople trained? They are trained to
overcome objections! That means one party — the seller —
wins, while the other party — the buyer — loses. This is the
wrong approach. Trying to overcome the objection will
cause the buyer and seller to lock horns in a confrontation,
leading to one party losing.

Okay, so Rule #1 is: breathe and relax.

Rule #2: Get Curious, Not Confrontational

What do I mean by "get curious"? Think about how you
must turn an objection into a win–win question. Ask
yourself, " What are three possible reasons why this person
just said what they did?"

If you don't get curious, you're never going to arrive at the
point where you can ask the correct questions; you'll be too
busy trying to protect your turf.

If you don't get curious and ask accurate questions, you're
likely to find yourself in an argument. When a seller is
involved in an argument with a buyer, most of the time the
seller will lose the sale.

Worse yet, even if the seller "wins" the sale, the buyer is not going to like or respect the seller afterward. In fact, the buyer will probably cancel the sale, or work to unravel it later post-sale. That means you make a successful sale to only a few versus many buyers.

So, Rule #2 is: Get curious. Don't get confrontational. Don't get offended. Get curious!

Just breathe, relax, and get curious.

Rule #3: Think Before You Act or Speak

Remember, get curious, not confrontational.

Then apply: think before you act.

Don't react and try to move forward. Take a moment to think about what you are going to say or do. Too many times I've seen sellers react without thinking and say things that cannot be taken back.

Even if the seller doesn't intend to be argumentative, when the buyer is in a heightened emotional state, the smallest thing can set them off and make them feel like they are in a fight.

When they feel like they are in a fight, they're going to try to take back certainty by shutting down the sale. At that point, the sale is harder to close and all but lost.

Rule #4: Ask Really Good Questions and Let Them Talk

Not all questions are created equal. Closed-ended questions typically only require a simple yes, no, or short answer. These questions don't reveal anything about the thought process or the underlying emotions of the other person you are seeking to communicate with for a successful sale. That's *not* what you want.

Here are some examples of closed-ended questions:

- Is that your final answer?
- Can I help you with that?
- Are you the only decision-maker?
- Would you like to give this a try?
- Is this the one of a kind of product you're looking for?
- Are you happy with your current supplier?

Open-ended questions, on the other hand, require more information and expression. These questions reveal the thought process and the underlying emotions. That's exactly what you want. You want the buyer to express where their fear is coming from.

Here are some examples of open-ended questions:

- How do you measure success?
- What do you perceive will be the five biggest challenges for you this year?

- Can you describe to me what it is like to be responsible for running your division?
- What are three of your least favorite memories of a salesperson you have worked with? And what are three of your most positive memories about a salesperson you have worked with?

To arrive at the heart of the matter, you need to initially ask good open-ended questions. You may have to ask a series of them. When you think before you act, you form those valuable questions.

But finding the real reason also requires letting the buyer talk and listening to what they say. Giving the buyer the opportunity to express what they are feeling goes a long way toward alleviating the problem. So, once you've asked a good question, don't rush to speak again. Sit back, breathe, relax, and be attentive to what they are saying.

Rule #5: Don't Overcome the Objections; Resolve Them

When you've asked the good questions and you're letting the buyer talk, listen for ways to resolve the issue, not overcome it.

Why? Because the buyer isn't looking to be overcome. That is what one does to win in a wrestling match. You pin your opponent's shoulders to the floor. In sales, however, the buyer usually isn't in fight mode if you follow the rules correctly as described in this section.

Insight: The buyer is looking for a resolution for their discomfort, for something that will allay their fears. As world-class entrepreneurs, sales conversion professionals, business executives, or even in our personal relationships, *we want to provide them with that solution.*

Rule #6: Focus Only on Win-Win

When we're trying to overcome things, we're focused on win-lose — someone is going to win, and someone is going to lose.

This is the incorrect approach, especially if you want a long-term client who repeatedly buys from you.

Instead, when we focus on win-win, we put ourselves on the buyer's side of the table and begin to see things from their perspective.

Remember, when the buyer wins and sees you as the positive influence in helping them resolve their fears and obtain the right product or service, then you win.

Rule #7: There Should Be No Loser

Lose-lose is not an option. Win-lose should not be an option, either. The goal is win-win.

We achieve win-win by asking questions and allowing the buyer to express themselves. We then help guide them —

not manipulate them — to a positive and effective resolution.

Sometimes, though, it may seem like you're losing because the conversation isn't going well. Don't worry, you're not losing.

You're not losing because, during the conversation, you're focused on gaining knowledge. The more knowledge you gain, the better prepared you'll be to ask more good questions and address their concerns. And if, during this discovery process, you find that the sale is not right for the buyer, then that is a win-win, too, because if you sell them something that is not in their best interest, they will probably return it due to buyer's remorse. Most importantly, you will miss the possibility to ever sell them or their friends, family, or business relationships anything in the future. So, if you find that the sales is not right, then you be the first to let them know that this is not in their or your best interest. You get to remain friends and they will respect you have integrity.

So again, don't be afraid to simply ask really good questions and listen. Talking often helps the buyer think and work things out. If you consistently interrupt that process, you're going to break rapport and find yourself in a fight.

Insight: Again, you may find while asking questions that this is not the right client fit for you. If so, take the high road and do the honorable thing by playing win-win and walking away from the sale. Remember that there's no loss unless you play win-lose. The biggest way to lose is to sell something to someone that they truly do not need or want to buy and cause them buyer's remorse. Buyer's remorse is the ultimate loss for you because the buyer is likely going to blame you, and then never buy from you again because you violated their trust.

Rule #8: Watch Your Tone and Expression

This is often easier said than done, but is a crucial piece of the process, especially when you are faced with the buyer's fears and objections.

Studies show that the words we use are of lesser importance compared to the vocal and body cues we use. That's not to say that words are unimportant; they definitely play a crucial role. But a lot can be said through tone of voice, facial expressions, and body language.

Just think about the word *no*. How many different emotions can we convey with that single word by altering the tone of voice and the facial expression? We can convey surprise, disgust, anger, irritation, happiness, and even exhaustion and surrender with just a small change in tone and a few tweaks of our facial muscles.

The way we say the words can mean much more than the words themselves.

Pay attention to achieving just the right tone for the situation, and that can go a long way in helping with the next step.

Rule #9: Maintain Rapport at All Times

Rapport is made up of three things:
- Trust
- Like
- Respect

Many will say that these three things are equally important. But from years of working with tens of thousands of clients, I believe that *trust* is the most important of the three. If I had to assign a percentage to each, it would be:

- 50 percent trust
- 25 percent like
- 25 percent respect

The reason trust is more important than like and respect is because when a buyer trusts you, they will be more apt to be open and forthright, giving more honest answers.

If the buyer likes you but doesn't trust you, they're going to hold back. If the buyer respects you but doesn't trust you, they're also going to hold back. Even if the buyer likes *and* respects you, but doesn't trust you, they're going to hold back valuable information that can help both of you.

But if the buyer likes you enough, respects you enough, and trusts you wholeheartedly, they will be open and give you direct, honest answers. When that happens, you are far nearer to closing the sale in a win-win fashion.

So, the way you turn an objection into a question is by paying attention to establishing trust, like, and respect.
You start by asking open-ended questions and looking for feedback. You then ask even more open-ended questions, and let the buyer express themselves so that they can share the real issue, or what I like to call the *Real It*.

The Real It is the real reason for the objection, but it may not be what the buyer initially tells you. Most of the time it's not. Because objections are emotions, and emotions are not always logical or well- defined, the Real It can be elusive. If you don't find it, resolving the objection is going to be difficult.

The real issue isn't that they don't possess the money or the time, or that they must talk to their partner. The real issue is fear. When you uncover the reason for their fear, you'll understand the Real It.

One last point about building rapport: start with asking open ended questions, and continue to ask more of them. This does not mean you cannot ask closed ended questions too, but be careful not to ask a lot of them, and never begin with one – except for something like, "Are you open to a question or two?" To initially practice, use the 80/20 rule as a guide and ask eighty percent open ended and twenty percent closed ended. As you get used to asking great questions, you will find the percentage that works for you with your buyers.

CHAPTER 7

HOW DO I KNOW WHICH OBJECTIONS TO EXPECT?

In this chapter, we'll learn:

Secrets to discovering the objections you'll hear before you sell your product or service

Before anybody — be they entrepreneur, business owner, or salesperson—starts to sell their product or service, they carry high expectations that *everybody* is going to want what they are offering.

The reality can be less accurate. And this sales arrogance is a breeding ground for objections to form. To avoid this, remember the following.

Key: The first thing you want to do before you even think about selling a product or service is to survey the target audience to learn what they think about what you're going to sell. If you talk to enough people, this interview process will uncover the objections you will encounter.

When you approach the survey participants, say things like, "I'm not attempting to directly sell you anything at this time. I am seeking your help and invaluable insight. I'm researching to find out what someone just like you is interested in and what you like and don't like about [insert product or service here]. Would you please give me no more than five minutes to help me, and answer three quick questions?"

Most people will say yes to that request, as they want to help someone, and yet, most salespeople do not first survey the audience to uncover the objections. Instead, they find themselves in a presentation being bombarded by objections for which they are completely unprepared. Just a bit of upfront research, and they would have been ready and could have addressed the objections before they were even voiced.

That brings us to an important question: how do you head off or diffuse potential objections?

Key: Address objections before and throughout your sales presentation.

You (the seller) should be the one to first raise objections, not the buyer. You do that by building the objections with the solutions into your messaging prior to and during your presentation.

For example, I know that *I need to talk to my partner* is a popular objection. Many years ago, I sold an introductory product that was $399.00. During my presentation, I would head off the *I need to talk to my partner* objection by telling the story about Business Partner A and Business Partner B.

Business Partner A exits the mall (or wherever) to find that all four of the tires on her vehicle have been slashed.

I would ask, "Does Business Partner A have to call Business Partner B for permission to invest $450 to buy new tires?"

Most of the time the response I would hear was, "No, she needs new tires now, so she calls the tire shop, buys new tires, and gets it done."

In a situation like this, I explain that this is a good lesson on how to effectively run a business. I relate that reliable statistics show that many businesses do not grow because their partnerships trip each other up by procrastinating on smaller decisions. Then, using statistics or a quote from a reputable source, I show them that the healthiest businesses are owned by business partners who trust one another to do the right thing on smaller decisions, and only need to confer on super-large ones.

After that story, I simply ask a good question to guide the buyer to agree that this is a likely scenario with a logical sequence and a positive outcome. If they agree, we move on; if not, I know that there is a fear there.

If you, as the seller, want to be at the top of your game, don't wing it. Rather, come prepared. Prepare ahead of time by proactively having stories, examples, and questions for objections you would likely encounter, and practice them beforehand so that they are natural responses. I do this, teach my clients to do so, and recommend you do the same.

By working these stories, examples, and questions into your presentation upfront, you will preempt most of these objections. Because the stories and examples show the buyer upfront what they may have feared, they rarely react with fear because there are no longer unknowns and occasionally if they do react with fear, you know this is something you must address.

So, find out what objections you could encounter during your presentation by surveying and asking questions of the potential audience before presenting to the potential buyer.

As an added benefit, conducting audience surveys and research might lead you to a previously unrecognized buying group. Imagine discovering a whole new buying market!

CHAPTER 8

HOW DO I DEAL WITH OBJECTIONS?

In this chapter, we'll learn:

How to handle objections like a pro

Developing a system for resolving objections means identifying which objections may come up *before* you go into your messaging or presentation.

Sit down and list all the objections the buyer could possibly pose, no matter how silly they seem to you. The better prepared you are, the more successful you'll be.

While you're doing this, keep in mind the reason buyers object: they're afraid and trying to regain some semblance of certainty.

Anytime humans' wants, needs, fears, or desires are *not* met, it creates a level of uncertainty.

Occasionally you may discover that even when their wants, needs, fears, and desires are met, there is *still* some level of uncertainty that presents itself.

Imagine, for example, that you are selling personal growth programs. To the buyer who really wants growth, the mere fact that they are going to grow can create a sense of uncertainty. Even though they view their personal growth as positive, there is uncertainty that is formed from the perceived process.

This uncertainty may cause the buyer to think: *My personal growth is important to me but what if I grow in my personal space and my spouse doesn't? I may end up divorced.*

They have imagined a future what-if scenario and have dragged that fear back to the present.

At the same time, they may remember a time when they tried personal growth training and did end up divorced because of it. Now they're pulling that fear from the past into the present, as well.

Whether it's the future scenario, the past scenario, or both, the fear will lead to an objection: *I've got to talk to my spouse before I do this.*

Your job as the seller is to anticipate and understand these objections. You can then address them and provide solutions in your presentation before the thoughts even enter the buyer's mind.

Take Me to Your Leader

When dealing with objections, you want to make sure that you're working with the decision-maker—the person who actually has the authority to release the money from their bank account into yours.

Decision-makers are always the best to talk to, but sometimes it's unclear who the decision-maker is. Sometimes, an influencer can look like (but not actually be) a decision-maker but still highly influences the true decision-maker's decision. Keep an eye out for these people and be wary of influencers. Include them in the conversation; do not exclude them. Try to deal directly with the decision-maker without upsetting or passing over the influencer. Sometimes, achieving this can be tricky.

Make sure you always address the objections of *both* the influencer and the decision-maker. Do not exclude the influencer; instead, try to understand how deep their influence is with the decision-maker and adjust your involvement with them per your assessment. Again, this can be a bit of a learning process, but it is invaluable for you to know — so please make a good effort.

For example, the person to whom you are speaking is an influencer, not a decision-maker, in the buying process. Would that make a difference in the response you receive?

Let's recall the example in the last chapter of Partner A and the slashed tires. Now imagine that Partner A is only fifteen years old.

It's relatively easy to see that the teen may be an influencer, and not the financial decision-maker. Would the answer you, as the tow-truck driver, give to their objections be slightly different than the one you would give to Partner B (the parents)?

Likely, the answer will be yes, as the teenager, being the influencer, must first say to the tow-truck driver, "I've got to talk to my parents first to get their credit card and permission." In most cases, it is common for a fifteen-year-old not to possess a credit card; however, it is becoming more common because credit card companies are allowing individuals under the age of eighteen to use a card under their parents' account so you as the seller must first ask.

The last sentence here brings a point, which is never assume that the perceived influencer is an influencer *only*. They may appear to be the influencer, but instead are the decision-maker (in this case, the teen has a credit card).

You discover this information by asking the right questions.

Insight: Not all objections are unwarranted.

Many of them are, in fact, absolutely valid.

Many times, no matter how high the need, want, or must-have of what you are selling, the influencer can't authorize spending without the permission of the decision-maker.

But that does not make them unimportant to the sale, as the influencer might exert such strong influence that they can knock out a sale if their objections are not addressed — even if they don't say a lot to the salesperson during the sales presentation.

For example, one day my wife and I went shopping for a new television. We entered a sizeable retail store and told the sales associate that we wanted a large-screen television.

The sales associate then proceeded to direct all his questions and comments to me, the man, while completely ignoring her. She spoke up, and said to the sales associate, "I'm here too, you know."

The sales associate acknowledged her, apologized, and within a couple of minutes, went right back to asking questions and directing comments to me alone.

I then instructed the sales associate to direct all questions and comments to both of us. He did so for about two minutes and then went back to focusing only on me.

Keep in mind, I wanted a new television. The units they had at this large retail store were what I was looking for and at my price point.

Additionally, I do not like to shop, so for me this was the perfect place to buy, and I wanted to buy at that time.

However, there was no way I was going to purchase from that sales associate or that location because the sales associate did not address my wife (who was a definite influencer) equally in the decision-making process.

I recalled past situations when other sales associates neglected to address her during the presentation and the conversation. Every time someone did that, she rightfully became upset and said, "I would never buy from or trust someone who neglects the partner in a relationship."

Because I want to keep our relationship strong and support her objections, I refuse to proceed with the sale.

Your job going in is to address the objections of the influencer and the decision-maker, even if you are only talking to one, the other or both at the same time.

If the influencer is not present during the sales presentation, you still want to address the concerns of the influencer. That will help settle the decision-maker because you are playing for a win-win.

If you accidentally present to an influencer without the decision-maker, don't beat yourself up for your mistake — it's usually a wasted effort so try not to do this if possible.

If you do, then you do want to make sure you create the opportunity to present to the decision-maker, too, and remember that the influencer can definitely help to close the sale because they are often highly influential.

By addressing all the objections, you make it a win-win for all parties involved.

Prepare to Stay in Rapport

Insight: Preparation is about understanding these three major points:

1. How to stay empathetic
2. How to continuously build rapport
3. How to give the buyer a pathway from negative emotions to the positive emotions associated with your product or service and with YOU

That's what this is all about.

Except when we are purposely trying to drive pain to serve the potential buyer, we take the buyer away from negative emotions, we build like, trust, and respect — the base components of rapport. When the buyer trusts you, they will tell you anything. They will go the extra mile. They will do the things that they wouldn't do for someone they don't trust.

Most sales companies inadvertently make it more challenging by teaching their salespeople to *Crush the objection, Overcome the objection, or Say [this phrase], and it will resolve everything for you.*

I once went to a timeshare presentation in Orlando, Florida. At the time, I wanted to buy Disney tickets, so I took them up on the offer to receive four free tickets to Disney in exchange for sitting through the presentation. I am a sales guy, so I was willing to stay open. Right before the presentation, I went to the men's room, and in that room, members of their sales team were gathered. I thought it a strange place to congregate and have a sales meeting but they were there and so was I.

I overheard several salesmen there saying things like: *Yeah! crush them! We're gonna take these sales today! We're gonna take him! We're going to get twenty-five! Boom. Boom. Boom. No matter what they say, we are gonna sell, sell, sell!*

I was standing right there next to them. I thought: *Who trained you? You are coming out to crush, but you don't have to, and I am the potential buyer listening to this. There is no way I would buy even if I love the offer. Rapport was broken.*

Our rapport was lost in that moment as they set the frame for me, the buyer, to lose. The sad part is that other sales strategies like this still sometimes work, but most of the time they don't work well because they are not addressing two critical elements present in every sale.

Insight: There are two needs in every single sale: the *business need* (your products and services to be delivered), which the "pre-determined sales formulas or pre-determined canned phrases" might support, and the *human need*.

That human need is defined by:

- The quality of feeling worthy
- Connection
- Love
- Certainty
- Emotions, such as self-acceptance and many others.

Too often, sellers address only the business need and completely miss the often more influential human need.

Prepare to Connect With People

Ask yourself this: *"To whom am I selling?"*

Common answers include CEOs, VPs, CFOs, board members, college students, teenagers, moms, dads, and grandparents. All of those answers are valid, but take away the title, and what are you left with? People!

So now, ask yourself again: *To whom am I selling?*

Insight: You sell to people who are human beings, not to titles or industries. You sell to people whose names just happen to be attached to titles or industries. Titles and industries can easily change. People, though, are far less likely to change their feelings or identity because these are developed throughout their life and are tied to their needs.

When a salesperson is taught to "crush objections," many times they've been taught to ignore the buyer's negative feelings. Doing this most times creates more fear and more negative feelings and results in more objections. When taught to crush the objection, the salesperson is learning to sell to the business need only.

The salesperson is *not* being trained to sell to both the business needs and the human needs of the prospective clients, who are, after all, just people—not titles and, without question, not industries.

By working to "crush objections" and push the negative feelings even deeper, the seller is creating additional uncertainty, which only leads to more objections and puts the buyer and seller in an antagonistic relationship.

What's more, the seller has now forever linked themselves to the buyer's negative feelings. And in doing so, the seller has likely lost the buyer's trust, which is exactly the opposite of what the seller set out to do.

By the above explanation, I think you can see that crushing an objection is something you absolutely *do not* want to do. Instead, you want to be perceived as positive and emotionally connected to the resolution of the problem. When that occurs, rapport goes up.

How Do You Prepare?

You prepare by asking yourself questions like:

- *What are the five most common objections that I'm going to hear from the decision-maker(s)?*
- *What are the five most common influencer objections that I'm going to hear?*
- *What does the decision-maker want and fear?*

After you've answered these questions, ask yourself: *What does the **influencer** want and fear?*

Once you've established those wants and fears, reorder them by priority. When you've done this enough, you'll be prepared to head off or align with the common wants and fears that come up during every presentation.

For example:

- *I don't have the time.*
- *I don't have the money.*
- *I want to think about it.*
- *I must talk to somebody else first.*
- *You're too expensive.*

Insight: You, the seller, should strive always to connect yourself to the positive rather than the negative. Preparation makes this easier. There is one other point, which is sometimes, you will have to ask a question that drives pain in order to get the buyer moving off their current fear state sticking point. Just make sure you are in high rapport when you do so as that will give the buyer the perception that you are truly on their side and the pain question will not be construed as you are manipulating or causing harm to them. In doing so, the pain question will not be a negative association to you, but rather you will be seen as a person who is positively aligned with the potential buyer's best interest.

CHAPTER 9

HOW DO I TELL IF SOMEONE HAS OBJECTIONS, OR IF THEY ARE JUST NOT INTERESTED?

In this chapter, we'll learn:

Discerning the difference between objections and lack of interest so you can respond accordingly

How do you tell if someone has objections, or if they're just not interested?

Simple. You ask them.

Insight: If you've built trust and enough rapport, you simply ask   the buyer if they have any objections or if they're not interested. For instance, "Is this issue a temporary roadblock, or are you just not interested?"

Remember, this is not a win-lose, it's a win-win.

If you push a buyer into purchasing something that is not good for them, buyer's remorse will likely kick in and they are going to either A) return the product or service, or B) buy the product or service and then never buy from you again. Personally, I think the latter possibility is worse. Sure, you've made the sale, and you'll collect your commission, but you've already lost any future sales and referrals you might have made with this buyer. *Ouch!*

The buyer now associates you, the seller, with both the negative emotions felt during the sales process *and* the negative emotions felt after the sales process, because you sold them something they didn't need.

My advice: Don't do this.

In addition to losing a customer, you also possibly run the risk of doing damage to the buyer's job, business, and reputation, as well as risking your own. When a sale goes as described above, the buyer is going to talk about you, and not in a good way. They usually tell many people, and sometimes they tell the whole world via social media and other forms on the internet. Do you want your reputation to suffer because of one win-lose sale?

You can avoid these problems completely by being direct and asking the buyer if they're objecting or if they're just not interested.

Finding the Real It

The other way of discerning between objections and lack of interest is to find the Real It: The "Real It" is the real reason behind the objection.

Not the emotion being expressed, but the underlying root of why it is being expressed.

Insight: When you are met with an objection, do not ignore the objection.

That may run contrary to what you were taught, because some people claim that you can just ignore objections, and they'll go away. Some do, but it's a small percentage. Plus, when the objection doesn't go away, and it's not addressed, the buyer is going to feel cheated that their concerns were not resolved.

You want to discover the heart of the matter — the Real It.

If you have built enough trust and respect, just ask the buyer what the Real It is. If you haven't built enough trust and respect, keep building it while you deal with the objection and try to figure out what the Real It is.

Insight: Identify the Real It and focus on it.

When you focus on the Real It, your goal is to do your best to achieve agreement with whatever it may be.

Why is this so important? Think about it in terms of a relationship between someone and their significant other. In the following example, I will discuss the dynamic between a husband and a wife.

If the wife brings up problems and tries to engage the husband in a dialogue, but the husband ignores or objects to the wife's concerns, bad feelings will fester and grow. This also happens if the wife does the same to the husband, and in either case, it could lead to unnecessary quarrels and long term to the end of the relationship.

During a sale, objections are no different. The buyer brings up problems and tries to engage the seller in a dialogue about the fears and discomfort they are experiencing. It could be about the product, the service, or anything else, which might include *you*. If these concerns aren't addressed, it could lead to the end of the relationship.

CHAPTER 10

HOW CAN I PERSUADE THEM TO "SELL THEMSELVES"?

In this chapter, we'll learn:

How to guide the buyer to positively answer their own objections

A common question every salesperson asks is: *Is it possible to guide the buyer to "sell themselves"?*

Yes, it absolutely is possible. You can use questioning to bring them to that point. If you ask good questions and help direct their answers in a win-win fashion, many times they will close themselves on the sale and be happy they did so. This is gratifying, especially when they thank you for helping them.

To accomplish this, when a buyer says, "I don't have the money," you follow the rules and ask questions. You don't ignore the objection. You don't crush it. Don't be cute about it. You deal with it head-on in a win-win manner.

And when I say, "deal with it head-on," I don't mean later in the presentation — unless you intended to tell them, the buyer, that you planned on covering that for them in greater detail later in the presentation. If so, ask them if it would be acceptable to them to delay the answer for a short period, so you can cover that for them in more detail later in what you are presenting. If they say yes, make a mental note and *do not* forget!

For most objections, deal with it immediately (or as soon as you can). Stop what you're doing and deal with that objection by asking questions.

Techniques for Asking Questions to Expose the Real It

How do you ask questions to expose the Real It?

The simplest way to respond to an objection is to take what the buyer said and repeat it as a question.

When the buyer says, "I don't have the money," your response might be something like, "Did I just hear you say that you don't have the money?"

Remember in Chapter 6 when we talked about tone of voice? This question is a prime example of making sure your tone is not confrontational or somehow derogatory. It's easy to ask that question in a way that would spark a whole host of negative emotions in the buyer's mind if your tone is not one of genuine concern for the buyer.

Now you've asked the first question in an attempt to reach the heart of the objection — the Real It. Regardless of whether the buyer answers with a closed-ended yes or launches into an open-ended, "Well, yeah, I did say that but I really meant [insert explanation here]," you're going to continue asking questions until you identify the Real It.

Be prepared to invest as much time as necessary at this point in the process because the Real It is the foundation of the objection. Don't be in a rush. If you rush the conversation, the buyer may feel like you are trying to manipulate them. Give the buyer time, because sometimes they're not aware that they're consciously objecting. Remember, the objection is usually an emotion being displayed as some behavior. Take the high road and help them work through it.

It's also imperative to keep in mind that objections are human emotions put into words, with the goal of regaining some impression of the certainty that has been lost during the sales process.

An important note here for you is that sometimes a buyer's objection is the Real It. For example, *I don't have the money* could be a legitimate objection. It's a real issue when they literally do not have the money. No amount of trying to crush that objection is likely to work but helping them resolve it can bring about new opportunities for a sale. In this case, for example, maybe you offer different terms or structure things differently.

Recently, I was talking with a family business, and they wanted my services, but their Real It was that they did not have the money. They were in a situation where the bank was inquiring about taking their home back, and they had just gotten their business revenues back to a place where they did not have to shut the business down. They were barely making ends meet with their current cash flow and had zero savings left.

Instead of crushing the objection, I got curious about ways to help them resolve it, and together we came up with some options for them. During that time of questions and answers, one of the family owners said, "I want to thank you, because everyone else we have talked with has either pressured us or walked away when we said we didn't have the money."

Insight: Pressuring potential buyers or walking away, unless it is for the benefit of the potential buyer, are examples of crushing an objection, and doing either without good justification or explanation to the potential buyer will result in a massive break in rapport.

When the family business owners told me about how past people tried to sell to them, they presented a good position for me. Now I was not simply in a sale, but in a conversation of conversion. As in many cases, it was a simple fix to get them the money. In this case, even though their personal credit score had taken a dip, their business credit was still good because they had not financially defaulted on anything. Because of this, they were eligible to apply for a business credit line and had decided to do so. We looked at a couple of sources, and at the time of this writing they are awaiting answers to see if they are approved. If they are approved, who is likely to retain their business?

The lesson here is: if possible, always think long term because many business owners with companies have struggled at one time or another in their business cycle and they will not forget you being kind and helpful.

So, sometimes a buyer's objection is the Real It, and at other times, it is about something else entirely, and thus the objection is not the Real It. In that case, to resolve the buyer's *I don't have the money* statement, follow the rules stated earlier and don't forget to breathe, relax, become curious, and think.

You might ask, "I'm a little confused and seeking your guidance. What does 'don't have the money' mean to you?" Are you completely out of money, maybe going out of business or just currently running tight on cash flow? You wait for the response, and then you ask another question.

Remember, objections are attached to emotions, so the buyer may not necessarily give you exactly what you want after the first question. They may need time to figure it out for themselves by talking things through.

You're helping them do this by becoming curious, not confrontational. You're relaxed. You're breathing. You're not worried about the outcome. You're going for a win-win resolution.

A great way to frame your questions is with compassion and curiosity: "I understand. You believe you don't have the investment right now. Could you please tell me, what do you perceive the investment looks like?"

Or you could pose another open-ended question, such as: "Could you please share your thoughts with me about [insert topic here]?" That's a great way to get a buyer talking.

The answer might be something like: "From what you've said, and based on my current income and expenses, I'm probably not going to be able to do this because I won't have the money."

Now you're getting somewhere. You're starting to discover the Real It.

Next is another question from you: "Do you see the value and want the solution we are discussing?" This is a powerful question and helps you discern an objection that can be resolved from a lack of interest, which usually can't be resolved.

Now imagine that the buyer says: "Yes, I do want it. I'm just not sure I can afford it."

You might respond: "I know I can provide a lot of value for you, and feel I understand what you're sensing because other people have sensed that as well. But we haven't talked about what the investment would be like yet, have we?"

I recommend that you then lead the conversation through more questions. I might continue: "So you say you don't have money at all. Are you completely broke?" This isn't as bad a question as it may seem if you have built enough rapport.

The conversation continues:

Buyer: No, no, I'm not completely broke.

Me: So, are you concerned about what the investment might be?

Buyer: Yes.

Here's where I can isolate the Real It.

Me: All right, thank you for sharing that. Other than finding a way to make this affordable for you, is there anything else in the way that would prevent you from moving forward?

The buyer is going to tell you: "Yes, there's something else," or: "No, there's nothing else,"

You just keep working with them, asking good questions until they say there's nothing else. Now you've probably gotten to the Real It. Now you can continue to move toward agreement and resolution.

Achieving Agreement

The next step would be to arrive at agreement.

You might ask: *So, assuming we resolve this for you in a way that is affordable and makes you feel great, would you be willing to move forward?*

If they say yes, you're now in agreement. If they say no, you go back and try to find the Real It again because, even though you thought you had it, you may be only close. If so, just keep trying. Remind yourself that you are dealing with humans and their quirky emotions, and you may just need to give it another try or two. In almost every instance, when you persist, you will find the Real It.

This cycle is repeated until the deal is acceptable to the buyer, and the sale is made.

Never Assume They Can't Afford It

To assume that a buyer can't afford what you're selling can be construed as an insult. And if a buyer senses an insult, you have broken rapport.

Also, when you assume, you inject your own beliefs and values. As we stated in the previous chapter, you can then invoke an objection by inviting it with your language, questions, and actions.

That's why it's so important to ask questions and find the Real It. Once you identify the Real It, you can resolve the issue by asking additional questions and guiding them to a decision.

In the hypothetical conversation above, when they said *I don't have the money and I cannot afford it,* I didn't tell the buyer *I command you to buy.* I asked questions to discover the Real It and helped them change their view, and once that was accomplished, I got into agreement with them.

I asked, "Is there anything else that would prevent you from moving forward?"

They said no.

"Okay, so if this is right for you, I will ask you to invest at the end. Are you okay with this?"

"Yes."

They are resolving their own objection at that point.

CHAPTER 11

HOW DO I WIN THEM OVER WITHOUT ARGUING?

In this chapter, we'll learn:

> How to persuade without arguing

This could be the shortest chapter in the book.

Insight: No objections should be argued. Ever.

Seriously, we could end this chapter right here. It should be clear that if you're in an argument, you're in a conflict with the buyer. An argument is usually perceived as a fight, and that is not good. Let me explain.

When you're arguing an objection, you are breaking rapport and once rapport is broken, you're going to lose, whether you make a sale or not. Most of the time, you'll lose that sale even if they initially say yes, as the buyer will, with high probability, undo it later.

Even if the initial sale is never undone, you eat only for a day and starve the business for the long term. Whether they initially buy or not, in most cases any future sales that might have been possible are gone. You will also lose goodwill and referrals.

Again, never argue an objection. You can debate and intellectually discuss it, but never argue, and in the process of the dialogue, *always*, *always* seek win-win.

How do you engage in overcoming objections without seeming argumentative?

Here's the answer: Always keep in mind that you're dealing with a human being who has feelings, wants, desires, needs, and fears, just as you do. To resolve objections without seeming argumentative, honor that person as an individual, and come from a human place, not just a business place.

The above makes the following insight pivotal to the sales process.

Insight: If you honor the buyer, and you know that they will be helped by what you are selling, then you have a *moral obligation* to help them resolve their objections.

No matter what the buyer says, you know you are honoring them when you tell them that they must buy your product or service because it's going to impact their life in such a positive way. You are convinced that you are doing the right thing — you are helping — and are on the moral high ground by providing the product or service. Just keep in mind that treating the buyer as a human being doesn't mean that you back down or walk away from the sale. It means you honor them even if you must go fifteen respectful verbal rounds with them to help them. If you are in high rapport, they will love you for it.

Help Them Resolve Their Own Objections; Make the Right Decision for Them

Your job is to help the buyer resolve the objection, and it is best accomplished by their own decision, with your guidance. *You* don't overcome it; you help them to resolve it for themselves. By helping them do so, you are now viewed as a helper, one who resolves problems, rather than an antagonist, one who overcomes or crushes problems.

Honor is, perhaps, one of the most important lessons you can learn from this text. When you honor the buyer as a valued human being, you are working to build rapport through respect, like, and trust.

Once you have established rapport, a buyer will do a lot of things that they wouldn't do when there is no or low rapport.

Many times, a buyer will purchase a product for no other reason than they trust the seller. Even if the buyer feels that it's a small percentage not the right fit, they will buy it because they trust the seller's judgment. The buyer trusts that the seller is working for a win-win and that the sale can help both parties. That sale is also justified in the mind of the buyer as a good decision even after the sale. The buyer trusted the seller, and if the seller sold with a moral obligation, it is a good decision for the buyer. It is a win-win.

Follow-Up Is Your Friend

Sometimes, even if the buyer's desire is high, they also have valid objections and a real reason that the sale cannot happen. It is not an immovable condition but a legitimate objection where the sale cannot happen right now. This is where you as the seller must stay in touch via follow-up.

For example, the timing can be wrong. This is a real and legitimate concern for the buyer if you are trying to sell them a house while they're in the middle of a divorce or a bankruptcy. The purchase can't happen because the timing is not right. That doesn't mean that a sale can't happen later, and that is why follow-up is so important.

Here are some other reasons:

Sometimes, there truly is no money in the budget at that time, and there won't be any money in the budget until next year. If you try to sell to a regulated government account, for example, they may not be able to spend money at that time of year. It doesn't mean they won't buy later; it just means that you need to follow up and stay with the buyer.

I have made sales that have taken two years to gain the initial purchase. Two years! After that, though, the same client purchased twenty more times within the next two years. As you can see, follow-up is key to maintaining rapport and gaining the sale.

So, don't make the mistake of thinking that all objections are somehow false. Come at the objection from a place of honor and try to find out what the Real It is.

As I write this book, I am in the process of a sale in which I must be patient. A doctor is committed to the purchase of $100,000 in business coaching and services, but the funds have not been released into my bank account. Why not?

Ten days ago, he learned that his wife was very ill. They have been in and out of hospitals, and they think that she may have kidney cancer. No doubt, this is going to affect him in a great way because he loves his wife. This is where honoring the human being comes into play. I have been following up, and my focus has not been 100 percent on the sale, but 90 percent on his wife's health and their mental state.   I received an email informing me that, in three days, the doctor will hear back from the oncologist regarding the wife's test results. If those results show she is free of cancer, the funds will be sent right away. If the results indicate she has cancer, the funds will not be transferred, and the doctor is going to spend time with his wife.

Some salespeople would've "crushed" the sale and attempted to bully this prospective buyer into committing the funds right away if they were afraid of losing the sale. When you're afraid to lose a sale, you're playing win-lose, not win-win. When we honor the buyer as a human being and put ourselves in their shoes, not from a place of being weak, but from a place of humility and strength, then we always win. Don't confuse being meek with being weak.

The Law of Averages

Part of understanding how to resolve objections is understanding the law of averages. This was explained to me by Mr. Russ Whitney. One day, I was complaining to Russ that I was frustrated and seeking to close a sale that I knew should be closed.

Russ asked, "Why are you so frustrated?"

I said, "Because I don't think the sale is going to close, but I know it should."

He replied, "It's a law of averages, Doug."

I whispered, "What is that?"

Russ then explained that, in every sale, there is a percentage that will close easily, some that will take time, and a percentage that will never — and indeed *should* never —

happen. If we track the results over time, those ratios will reveal themselves to us.

The sales that we must twist and wrestle to the ground are usually sales that we should never have closed anyway because the likelihood of them sticking is low. The sales that make us use unethical tactics to close should simply never happen.

Using the law of averages means that you detach yourself from the outcome of the sale and become free to focus on what you should do. You can honor the buyer as a valued human being and focus on the buyer's needs, wants, and must-haves.

When you do this, you are selling through humility, which is powerful. Again, don't confuse meekness with weakness.

Meekness is when you do the right thing by the buyer and build trust.

Weakness is when you metaphorically wrestle the buyer and crush their objections to win the sale.

If your intent is to be meek and to grow trust, you'll be able to work out anything with your client.

Once you develop trust, you help them buy if it's right for the buyer. You use your moral obligation to make sure that you do everything you can to help them consume your product or service because it is right for them, all while keeping the law of averages intact.

If these last few paragraphs make you feel a little queasy or anxious, that likely means you do not have enough prospects to present to, and that is another challenge which is easily resolved by creating an overabundance of new potential buyers for yourself. When you do, you will never be anxious about the law of averages again.

CHAPTER 12

HOW DO I TURN OBJECTIONS INTO AGREEMENTS?

What we'll learn:

The art of getting agreement

I've trained tens of thousands of people in the *hows* and *whys* of improving sales conversion. People often ask, "Doug, if I'm not supposed to overcome objections, then how do I learn this art of turning objections into agreements?"

I'm so glad you asked.

Insight: You're going to work through the steps of dealing with an objection, qualifying it, isolating the Real It, helping to resolve the process and then confirming it to make it a win-win for all involved, and finally, *practice* until it becomes a habit.

Most people mess up by either dabbling with the method or making it too complicated. It's not complicated if you make it a system for yourself and learn to own the method of how to turn objections into agreements.

Objections will happen because it all comes back to the same core: You're dealing with people. Dealing with people requires that you honor them and use the system you're learning here.

People across all cultures are generally the same. Yes, they live by different values. They raise their children differently. They think differently.

But when it comes to selling — and I've dealt with many people in many different companies and geographical regions — I've discovered that people all over the world want the same things. People want love. They want desire. They want to feel that they can contribute in some way. They want to feel that they matter. They want to make a little bit more money than they need. They want to obtain a better quality of life. They want their children to have better lives than they had growing up. They want to help others.

When you, as a seller, realize that you're dealing with a person, and not solely a title, such as CEO or CFO. When you do, you'll be able to create some incredible win-win situations.

Remember that a title is just a title. The person behind that title is usually just as afraid as you are. They are concerned they are going to make a mistake, concerned they are going to let their company down, concerned of being fired. They know that they are only there because they did a good job and were given the letters in their job title that set them apart from everyone else. And from their perspective, you will never take those letters away from them. If you, the seller, do anything to try, you are going to create discomfort for them.

To allay that fear and to create the win-win situations, you must help them dig down to the Real It on which all the objections are built and help them resolve that Real It so that they feel good about it.

Let's look at an example.

Insight: I have built huge buying relationships with people who have said: *I don't have the time right now.*

Let's say I'm selling to a CFO who, initially unbeknownst to me, is going through a divorce or an IRS audit. There I am, just by selling to her, likely throwing one more "problem or thing to think about" into the mix, and the CFO is feeling overwhelmed.

So, *I don't have the time* is not the real objection. But by digging down to the Real It, I discover that she's got a lot to deal with right now and can't focus on what I want, which is the sale. Time is not the Real It; focus seems more plausible, but the Real It is her feeling that relates to her inability to focus.

I help her work through what she is dealing with, and maybe my proposed sales solution will help resolve that, or maybe it will not. Either way, I do the best I can, and I am not afraid to be the first person to walk away from the process if it is not right; I'm not afraid because I'm honoring the buyer. That's a powerful idea.

Insight: Don't be afraid to be the first to walk away from the sale if the sale is not the right thing for the buyer. This serves both of you and allows you to conserve your time to work with those that will buy.

Now, other people will teach different methods. Most will say that you just stay in there and keep emotionally beating and pounding on them. The reality is that the strategy of endless attack does work on a small percentage. But that percentage is dwindling every day.

With the advent of the internet and the plethora of choices that it brings, buyers are looking for the human connection they can't get from a machine or a person who acts like a callous mechanism.

Complex sales, in fact, demand a human connection. And if you make that human connection and add honor to it, you'll be in an excellent position to find a win-win for all involved.

If you're not honoring the buyer, you're creating a difficult situation in which discovering the Real It may be next to impossible. And getting to the Real It and resolving it is the whole point of the process.

CHAPTER 13

WHAT FORMULA CAN I USE TO DEAL WITH OBJECTIONS?

In this chapter, we'll learn:

> One of my methodologies to handle any objection.

Once you understand what the real objection is the "Real It" many sellers find that they're stuck asking questions without the ability to move out of that phase and into the next step. That's when my formula comes in handy.

The 3QAQRQ Formula:

Q-Q-Q-A-Q-R-Q

That stands for Question-Question-Question-Answer-Question- Reward-Question. Here's how it works for you.

Suppose that the buyer is saying: *You know what? We already work with a provider. We're doing business with them. We're very happy. We don't need you.*

At this point, many salespeople just walk away. They're done.

But you don't have to walk away. Remember: relax, breathe, get curious. Ask a question.

First, Build a Sandwich

No, I'm not talking about lunch, I'm talking about the sandwich technique. The sandwich technique is nothing new; it's been around for years, perhaps as long as there have been salespeople. It basically states that you surround whatever it is you're going to say with compliments, like the pieces of bread in a sandwich. These compliments make your words more palatable and easier to swallow.

I didn't make up the sandwich technique, but I embrace it because it works.

So, before I arrive at my formula, Q-Q-Q-A-Q-R-Q, I put a compliment on the front: C-Q-Q-Q-A-Q-R-Q.

It might go something like this:

You know what? I appreciate you telling me that. Most people would never tell me the real truth. I appreciate you being a professional and allowing me not to continue to invest a lot of time here trying to persuade you on something that you're happy with. I get it. Thank you, I appreciate it.

Once I've complimented the buyer, I can get to the center of the sandwich — what I really want to talk about.

Here's where I apply the methodology and work my way through **Q-Q-Q-A-Q-R-Q**.

After my compliment, I say: *"May I ask you a question?"*

The buyer is going to say *sure* 99.999 percent of the time.

I've got permission, so off I go.

The Q - Questions

I ask my first question: "Would you tell me one thing your current supplier is doing well?"

The buyer responds: "Oh, yeah, sure. They're on time and they provide me the reporting I need."

I ask my second question, sandwiched by compliments: "Okay, great. Thank you so much." (Compliment,

compliment, compliment.) "What's one thing you think they can improve on?"

Buyer: "Well, even though they're on time and they provide reports, their communication is not all that great. And now that I think about it, they are rather expensive."

Ah! They just gave me an opening. Now I see a few ways to start a conversation.

That takes me to my third question: "If you could find a company that delivered on time, provided great reports, communicated well, and was more affordable, would that be a package you would consider?"

If you can give them what they're getting now plus what they're not getting in a nonthreatening way, most of the time their answer is going to be yes. Let's assume it is yes, and if so, the next step is to give them the answer.

The A - Answers

"Well, I guarantee you that we provide those types of services, and we can absolutely hit this pricing."

The Next Q - Question

Your next question could be: "What else besides these two things (communication and pricing) would you want in an ideal scenario? In other words, if I could give you everything you were looking for, including on-time delivery, great reports, excellent communication, and lower pricing, what would that perfect scenario look like for you?"

The buyer will likely think for a few moments, and then say: "I think it would look like what you said, plus [this and this and this]."

Alright! Now we're getting somewhere. Bring on the rewards.

The R - Rewards

"Thank you so much. I really appreciate you for helping me here. I know we can absolutely give you what you're looking for."

Notice that I've just rewarded the buyer with compliments and the possibility of receiving everything they want. Now it's time to ask another question.

The Next Q - Question

"Can we set up a second meeting to investigate this deeper? Or would you like to discuss more now?"

"Sure, let's take time to discuss it right now while you are here," they say.

Or they say, "Sure, when would you like to meet?"

Either way, you are now closer to bringing your products or services to their company, and you didn't need to beat them up or crush their objection to do so.

Insight: It doesn't matter how many questions you ask or how many rewards or answers you give, just make sure you do not overdo it on you giving answer after answer as they will be in control of the conversation or on the rewards or you may seem disingenuous. For now, though, we return to the sandwich technique, and our last piece of bread, which is the compliment.

You: I really appreciate your trust and faith in our conversation and in me. Would you consider doing business together?

The buyer: Absolutely. You made me realize that I'm overspending.

Of course, no matter how great of a job you've done, there is always a risk that the buyer may go back to their supplier hoping they will match your offer. However, this is a low risk, if you use your sales skills and tie it down to make sure that this doesn't happen. The way you accomplish this is to ask a simple question to reaffirm what you do strongly in a positive way, so that the mindset of the buyer is that they want you versus their current supplier, or the worst-case scenario is that they want both of you.

Either way, you are ahead. The bottom line is that you made a connection, got them to realize that they were overpaying (which is value), and the door is still open for you.

Before ending the meeting, collect more information and set an agenda with next step expectations so you're prepared for next time.

Again, there are all kinds of scenarios that could come up, but the important thing is to stick as closely as possible to the 3Q-A-Q-R-Q formula sandwiched between compliments, C-Q-Q-Q-A-Q-R-Q-C.

The Greatest Technique Is Honor, Authenticity, and Trust

Beyond formulas, beyond techniques, beyond secret sauces, three things remain the foundation of any good sales presentation: honor, authenticity, and trust.

Insight: It is absolutely critical that you honor the buyer and make sure they understand that you're working toward a win-win.

It is absolutely essential that you remain authentic, so the buyer knows you and who you represent.

And, it is absolutely vital that you gain the buyer's trust.

You can use any number of sales techniques, but if you aren't connected to them in a positive, trusting way — because you haven't developed that kind of relationship — most everything you do will feel like manipulation.

That's why I don't teach a ton of slick techniques when handling objections. I've used techniques from other folks before — sometimes they work and sometimes they don't. But if I first establish that human- to-human connection (which contains trust, like, and respect) and then use the techniques with honor and authenticity, the buyer doesn't feel manipulated, even if they disagree with what I am proposing.

Insight: Questions are the lifeblood of any conversation.

The flow of the conversation is controlled by the flow of the questions you ask. Don't let the conversation wither and die. Ask plenty of high-quality questions and make them relevant to what you want to accomplish.

CHAPTER 14

WHAT YOU KNOW NOW — FINAL THOUGHTS

You now know the basics of how to handle objections without crushing them.

The insights in this short read are distilled from a lifetime of practice with this sales technique, as well as countless hours teaching and learning from my clients over the years.

This experience has helped me to see that objections are not the end of the sales process. In fact, they can be just the beginning — the beginning of a dialogue that can help you and the buyer reach a win- win situation and a lifetime relationship of repeat sales. All you need is to view their objection from the right perspective using a few honest, authentic, and rapport-building methods, and to put yourself in the right frame of mind.

Remember, you are not psychologically manipulating the person. Rather, you are being honest and authentic. You're building trust, like, and respect while using the proven systematic approach contained within this book.

The purpose of it all, of course, is to close more sales, help more people, enhance your business life, and perhaps your personal life as well. So, please, use whatever you can from this book to make that dream a reality.

I firmly believe that a big part of success — in business and in life — lies in honestly helping others achieve their goals. It's a win-win.

Recommendation: Study this material and practice what you have learned multiple times. Trying these techniques only once will not be enough for you to integrate them and apply them as second nature in your sales. Read this book repeatedly and practice what you have learned until you have mastered the techniques and methodology. When you're finished, I encourage you to pass this book on to someone else or, better yet, encourage them to go invest in their own copy, so that they can benefit from learning how to resolve objections.

And, yes, I will sell another book. (Never be shy about asking for the next sale.)

Best wishes and thank you very much for being my customer.

ABOUT THE AUTHOR

Doug Brown has led award-winning, high-performance teams and pioneered profitable development programs for companies. He has advised companies such as Intuit, CBS Television, Procter & Gamble, Enterprise Rent-A-Car, Nationwide, Embassy Suites, Inc, companies that are on the Inc. 500 to 5000 list of fastest growing companies, and thousands of other businesses and entrepreneurs.

Doug started working for his family business at the age of three and has gone on to found or build thirty-four businesses, including a telecommunications consulting company, real estate investment firm, SEO venture, entertainment business, and many more. Through his personal experiences and studies, he has developed a unique methodology for increasing revenues that is transferrable to any company. He specializes in helping companies acquire, convert, and lock in clients for life.

Doug has also been employed by multibillion-dollar companies and earned many top sales professional awards for his sales performances.

While employed as an independent division head responsible for creating, training, and presenting high-impact, results-oriented web seminars for the likes of Tony Robbins and Chet Holmes, Doug increased division sales by 864 percent and close rates by 62 percent in just six months.

He has also worked with Russ Whitney and trained clients of Jay Levinson, and numerous other trainers and businesses.

For four decades, Doug has studied business principles and self- development, passing on his knowledge and experience in order to serve others by helping their businesses grow.

His newest ventures are Business Success Factors, a business training company where he is the founder and CEO and Vibitno.com, which is a cloud-based, sales-acceleration software that helps business all around the globe.

Doug lives in New Hampshire.

For further information, please call 603-595-0303 or email at doug@businesssucessfactors.com.

Contact Information: Business Success Factors

20 Portsmouth Avenue, Suite 147, Stratham, NH 03885
Email: doug@businesssuccessfactors.com

Websites:
Businesssuccessfactors.com
Vibitno.com

PLEASE RATE MY BOOK

I'd be honored if you would take a few moments to rate this book on Amazon.com.

A five-star rating and a short comment ("Great read," or "Enjoyed it!") would be much appreciated. Longer, positive comments are great as well.

If you feel like this book should be rated at three stars or fewer, please hold off posting your thoughts on Amazon. Instead, please send your feedback directly to me so that I can use it to improve the next edition. I'm committed to providing the best value to my customers and readers, and your thoughts can make that possible.

You can reach me at doug@businesssuccessfactors.com.

With gratitude,

Doug

Made in the
USA
Middletown, DE